D1644293

'Jo was always going through her old boxes
of photographs. This book is a great way
of letting them see the light of day.'

Ronnie Wood

'I met Jo in 1980 and we had the best of times.
She showed me all the ropes when I first
went on tour. We were like sisters and Keith
always thought of Ronnie as a little brother.
We have crazy wonderful memories of being
on tour with the Stones, travelling the
world and raising children. We are still one
big family today.

Feels like yesterday. Well done Jo!'

Patti Hansen

Stoned

Photographs & treasures from
life with the Rolling Stones

JO WOOD

CASSELL
ILLUSTRATED

This is dedicated to all those I've toured the world with and love,
and to my children for accepting and loving me unconditionally,
and to all my grandchildren. I love and adore you all.

LIBRARIES NI
WITHDRAWN FROM STOCK

LIBRARIES NI
WITHDRAWN FROM STOCK

Contents

★

Introduction

I've always loved taking photos. Wherever we went, I always liked to carry a camera, and I've always been a bit of a hoarder as well, constantly putting stuff that I thought was interesting to one side. When I was taking photos, I didn't ever think they'd be published one day. I was just taking pictures of friends and family, but as time went by I used to think, 'Maybe one day I'll do something with all this.' I never quite got around to it but I never threw anything away either. We moved from LA to New York to London and my increasing stash of photos and mementoes travelled around the world with us.

A few years ago, I took a lot of things out of storage and there in the boxes were all these photo albums. I was a bit scared of delving into them at first. There was album after album. I couldn't tell you how many photos I have – it must be thousands – but I started to look through them. It made me realize what an incredible life I've had, how there were lots of people in the photos who were no longer here and I started to think, 'Maybe now is the time for a scrapbook that collects all this stuff.'

To be honest, I also thought, 'If I don't do this now, then one day, when I'm not here, what's going to happen to it?' I didn't want my kids to throw it out because they thought it was old junk!

Ronnie and I are friends, so I spoke to him about the book. I told him that I saw it as a celebration, a love letter to that time in my life. He was very supportive. The nice thing about putting together this book is it feels like it's an appreciation of the life I've had and closes off a chapter in my past. I hope it also gives people an insight into life on the road, what it was really like to be on tour with the Stones. We didn't have Instagram then, but to me it's like Instagram for the '70s, '80s and '90s!

It's funny to think how different life was back then. A lot of the time I was the only person in the room with a camera. Now everyone carries a phone in their pocket, which isn't always a good thing. Then there were

no such things as mobile phones, social media or selfies. I think you can tell that from the pictures because everyone is 'off duty', and the pictures are really natural and not posed. They just show what our life was like. These days people know someone can post a photo on Twitter or something like that, so they're probably a bit more guarded.

In fact, back then everyone was quite pleased when I pulled out a camera because it meant I could capture the moment – most of the people I was taking pictures of would certainly never take their own photos. I felt a bit for Mick. I think he had his photo taken so often he could live without it, but the rest of the Stones never minded.

In the early days I used a Polaroid, the instant cameras that would print the photo there and then. They were great because you used to watch the film develop into a picture in front of you – they were as close as we got to an iPhone. The only problem was that you didn't get a negative, which meant if you lost the picture, it was gone forever. I shudder to think what I've lost in transit.

Not long after we started going out, Ronnie ended up buying me a 'proper' camera. I took it everywhere with me, and I was taking so many pictures that Ronnie started to call me the Shutterbug. He even used that name as a credit on one of his solo records.

I didn't develop the rolls of film when we were on the road in case I lost them or gave them away, so I used to stick them in a big bag as we went. It was easier for me to just gather them up and keep them safe. The only problem was I was taking a lot of pictures – I have diaries from when we'd just got back from being on tour with notes saying, 'Take 105 rolls of film to be developed.' I used to have plastic carrier bags full of film canisters and I'd drag them to the processors who'd look at me like I was completely insane. It was probably quite mad for the developers printing these pictures, expecting them to be somebody's holiday snaps but suddenly realizing they're looking at the Rolling Stones and their mates. I made sure I used photographic shops that I trusted because, obviously, there was all sorts of stuff going on in the pics.

I don't really know where the passion for taking photos came from. I think I needed to do something on the road, and I liked being the

Shutterbug. They weren't the best pictures but they were a snapshot of a time. I just wanted to capture everything we were seeing.

I'd been in front of the camera as a model, so it was fun to have a camera myself and be the one taking the photos. I didn't realize at the time that what I was capturing was unique or that it was such an important part of my life. It was just fun. Keith's wife Patti used to take pictures as well – there were so many amazing moments to photograph.

Now, with the passing of time, I can see what an incredible world I was a part of. Interesting people were drawn to the Stones, and there was always a blur of stars around them. It was just normal for our kids that Brad Pitt was backstage – they didn't know any different. The thing with the Stones was there were always a lot of parties, and in every city we went to there was something happening. Everyone came to the shows, and the big cities like LA and New York were always crazy.

The Stones have had so many books published about them, lots they probably didn't like, but this one has been put together with such love on my part. (Saying that, I had so much stuff that I couldn't include everything. One thing I didn't squeeze in was an empty wrap I found in my diary from 1981 that said, 'One gram of Merry Xmas.' I won't say who wrote that. See if you can guess…)

I'm not massively nostalgic – I tend to look forward – but it's weird in some ways when I look at the pictures that it feels so long ago, like a totally different life, and yet sometimes it can feel like yesterday.

Ultimately, this book captures a unique time for all of us and I really hope this shows a side to the Stones that's never been seen before. The Stones organization is a big machine but within it is a family – and that's what you see in this book. There are friends in there who are no longer with us, people like Bobby Womack and John Belushi, but I just feel so lucky to have met them and lived the life I have. I don't look at their pictures and dwell on feeling sad that they're gone. I just think of how much fun we had. I've always had a pretty positive outlook and you have to think about the good times.

So this is a chance to pay tribute to lots of people who meant a lot to me and to say thank you for my extraordinary life.

WEDNESDAY

Morning

Read

Lunch

Afternoon

Collect Comp.
C.R's

The Early Years

★

It was fashion that changed my life. I grew up in a little place called Benfleet in Essex. It was only 30 miles east of London but to me, growing up quite a shy little girl, it felt like a different world from the Swinging Sixties happening on the King's Road and Carnaby Street.

I was the first of four children. My Mum was five months pregnant when she married my Dad and, while I didn't realize it when I was growing up, I know now it was hard for them when we were kids. Mum came from South Africa and was mixed race, which back then led to some disapproval. Dad didn't care. He adored her. Dad always loved collecting Lambretta scooters and Mum had a huge collection of dolls. I think my passion for collecting things must run in my genes.

I hated school. I went to a convent where teaching was basically nuns shouting at you, but I was always creative and, as I grew up, I became more and more interested in clothes.

My mother was very fashionable. I remember when I was only about seven seeing her in a brown check pencil skirt, paired with this chic jacket and brown suede stilettos, and thinking, 'My Mum looks so amazing.' Then along came Twiggy and Mary Quant and Biba and I became obsessed with fashion.

The only way to find out about fashion then was magazines. I was obsessed with buying them, and because my Mum was a great seamstress, she could make the clothes the models were wearing.

Then, when I was 12, I decided to try doing my eye make-up like Twiggy. I put on black eyeliner, did my lashes, looked in the mirror and thought, 'Wow!' When I came downstairs, my Auntie Lily was there. She looked at me and said, 'My goodness, doesn't she look pretty.' Up until then I'd never thought of myself as pretty – these days everyone tells their kids how gorgeous they are, back then they didn't – but once I put the black around my eyes, my life changed. Forty years on, I still love wearing that black eyeliner.

The minute Auntie Lily said I was pretty, I knew what I was going to do. I was going to be a model. In fact, I have a schoolbook and in it I wrote, 'I'm going to go up to London, have a flat in Knightsbridge and be a model.' I remember the girls in my class found it and when I went into school one day, they were reading it and they all laughed at me. The teachers thought I was being ridiculous as well, talking about being a model, but I thought, 'I'll show you.' It just gave me more determination.

I might have been shy but I was a strong person. Maybe I was resilient because my parents were quite strict and had taught us to be independent. I was able to cook a roast dinner by the time I was nine and I was always looking after my brothers and sister because I was the oldest.

My parents were right behind me, and my Mum helped me get onto a modelling course when I was 14. She also made all the clothes I needed for my graduation show.

Legally, I had to wait two years before I could join an agency's books because you had to be 16 but, in the meantime, I started to go out with a guy who had a boutique called The Ragged Priest. I used to love that name. The boutique was full of '70s fashion, like flares and Afghan coats, and seemed so exciting. We used to go up to London in his Morris Minor to buy clothes for his shop and I started to see how the fashion industry worked. I just loved it. London was so exciting and, as soon as I hit 16, I started to travel up there and joined my first model agency.

It was amazing. I wasn't earning a lot but I absolutely loved it. Thinking about it now I must have been so determined. I didn't know anyone in the fashion industry but I really wanted to be a model.

My agent would send me to casting after casting. I think it really helped that it didn't affect me if I was told I was too young, too short or even not sophisticated enough.

If I wasn't right for the job, that was okay, and I didn't make a song and dance if I wasn't the girl they wanted. I just went onto the next interview, whereas lots of girls were really sensitive about rejection.

I met my first husband, Peter, when I was 17 and a half. He was older, really flash and, suddenly, I was scooped up into this whole other world of restaurants and Bentleys and visiting the south of France. My life was moving so quickly, and before I knew it, I was pregnant. I stopped working to become a mum, but we had split up by the time I was 20.

It wasn't working, so I packed my bags and left, with my darling son Jamie in my arms. We went back to my parents and started again. I have had to do that a few times in my life.

Looking back, I was so young. I told my Mum, who had warned me I was making a mistake, that she was right and I cried my heart out. My parents were amazing. Mum did say, 'I told you so,' but she also said that she'd look after Jamie.

If my Mum and Dad hadn't helped me, I don't know what I would have done with my life. Everything would have been different, but with their support I was able to start modelling again.

I lived up in London during the week with my good friend Sue, working as hard as I could but having great fun as well. I remember being out, having only one hour's sleep and then turning up to a job. I must have been reeking of alcohol but when you're young, you can get away with it.

We were being naughty and running around London. We loved music and clubbing at places like Tramp. We used to pretend we were sisters and introduce ourselves as Phelia and Lickia Balls for a laugh. I remember one bloke just looked at me and said, 'Who's ever going to go out with a mad woman like you?' I thought to myself, 'Oh no,' but then I met Ronnie...

Early modelling

Here's my first diary from when I started working as a
model. I was 16. There's also the certificate I got from my
first modelling academy when I was only 14. I was so proud
and determined to be a model. In the middle is a picture of
my first child Jamie, who was such a good-looking baby.

1971

WEDNESDAY

Morning

6.15 Robert Montgomery
Book 3 New Burlington S.
W.1.

46 Abingdon Rd W.8.
Clive Arrowsmith

Afternoon

Norman Leman x2
Chrysler Bayswater Hotel
Kingh...

Paul Anthony → Everett Adv
10, Greycoat Place
W.1.

NOVEMBER 1971
S   1   7   14   21   28
M   2   8   15   22   29
T   9   16   23   30
W   3   10   17   24
T   4   11   18   25
F   5   12   19   26
S   6   13   20   27

PHONE : STUDIO
274 8865

HARRY JACOBS (PHOTOGRAPHERS) LTD.
152 LANDOR ROAD · STOCKWELL · S.W.9

PHONE : HOME
274 6876

On the catwalk

A very proud moment, walking the catwalk for
the first time when I was 14.

17

Modelling cards

I dug out these old modelling cards, which were used
to get jobs. You'd leave them with photographers in the
hope of getting an assignment. I used the name Howard
professionally because it was my Dad's middle name.

Jo Howard

Height 5'6½
Bust 33 Waist 23 Hips 34
Dress size 8-10
Shoes 5 Gloves 6½
Inseam 32 Outside Leg 42
Hair Blonde Eyes Blue

Grösse 1.69
Oberweite 84 Taille 58 Hüfte 86
Konfektion 36-38
Schuhe 38 Handschuhe 6½
Schrittinnen 81 Schrittaussen 107
Haare Blond Augen Blau

BOBTON's
40 Kings Road London SW3 4UD
Tel 01-589 2771/584 4397
Telex 22880

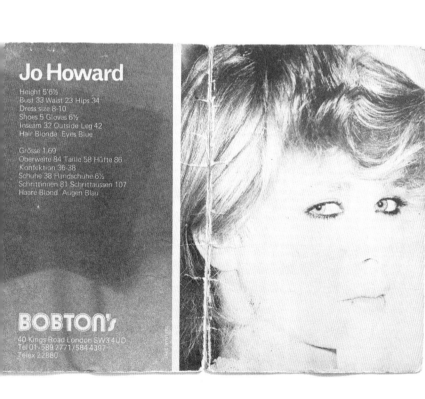

The Stones in '66

Left: While clearing out some boxes, I came across this old newspaper from 1 January 1966.

Below: The matador's jacket that Ronnie wore when he was with the Faces. He would always say how heavy it was to wear on stage. It used to have a matching pair of trousers.

Ronnie joins

Right: Another paper I found in the same box. This is from '75, the year that Ronnie joined the Stones for a tour of North and South America. He joined the band permanently the following year.

Below: A t-shirt that Ronnie gave me from the same year.

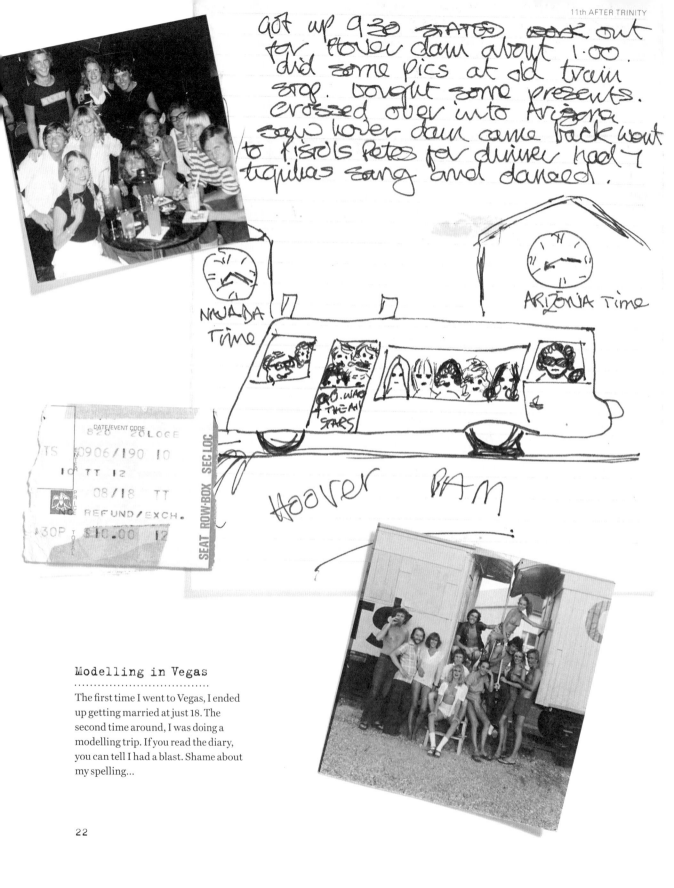

got up 9.30 started look out
for Hover dam about 1.00.
did some pics at old train
stop. bought some presents.
crossed over into Arizona
saw hover dam came back went
to Pistols Petes for dinner had 4
tequilas sang and danced.

NEVADA Time

ARIZONA Time

I.O. WAD
4 THEM
STARS

Hoover DAM

Modelling in Vegas

The first time I went to Vegas, I ended
up getting married at just 18. The
second time around, I was doing a
modelling trip. If you read the diary,
you can tell I had a blast. Shame about
my spelling...

First taste of the band

I went to this gig with my first husband, Peter. I wasn't that into the Stones, to be honest. In fact, I left halfway through because I thought it was too loud!

SATURDAY, MAY 22, 1976

WHAT A GAS! THE GREATEST SHOW ON EARTH COMES ROLLING BACK

EVENING NEWS R 3

STONED!

17,000 Londoners get high on Jagger's carnival of rock

By JOHN BLAKE
Pictures DAVID THORPE

Mick Jagger showing the form that had fans roaring for more

THE Rolling Stones hit London like World War III.

Their concert at Earl's Court—the most exciting yet, as they promised—began with the sound of cannon fire, a military bugle and wartime-like searchlights.

The Stones turned Earl's Court into a flag-draped, dazzling magical place for the first London concert in a British tour which is costing £1 million to produce.

The probing searchlights picked out an soft multi-coloured silk dragon suspended over the 17,000 fans.

Then they focused on the five petals of a giant 30ft.-high, 100ft.-wide black, gold and silver lotus flower that stood where the stage should have been.

Slowly the petals lowered and Mick Jagger was revealed in a skin-tight turquoise suit.

Then Keith Richard, Ronnie Wood, Bill Wyman and Charlie Watts, backed by Billy Preston and Ollie Brown came into view, and the unmistakable chords of Honky Tonk Woman hit the air like rifle fire.

The Stones built up a super-powered wall of sound with If You Don't Rock Me and Get Off My Cloud and then played a couple of numbers from their new album Black and Blue.

The whole night had a sensational carnival atmosphere.

The concert proved once again—if proof were needed —that the Stones are the greatest show business act in the world and London was glad to have them back for the first time in three years.

HIGH SPOT

They thundered through their hits and strongest album tracks until Can't Always Get What You Want when Mick Jagger persuaded the overawed audience to join him in singing the choruses.

Keith Richard, in skin-tight leather jeans and white T-shirt, was in better form than I have seen him for years, and his singing of Happy was one of the night's high spots.

Mick Jagger swung on his Tarzan rope further and higher than before.

And, after Midnight Rambler, Brown Sugar and other classics that have turned the Stones into living legends, they pumped confetti over the audience and threw buckets of water over the heads of those nearest the stage.

TIPPED OUT

Then Mick—by this time naked to the waist—emptied a bucket of water over his own head.

The stamping, dancing audience dragged the Stones back for the first encore I've seen them give.

They chose Sympathy for the Devil and as they sang 50 people dressed as carnival characters like Humpty Dumpty, sex goddesses and gorillas, danced on to the stage.

And finally the petals of the lotus flower were lifted as the Stones played on, and it really was over.

Later all the Stones except Keith sipped Coke with stars, including Lulu, Susan Hampshire and Patrick Mower, at the Cockney Pride Tavern in Piccadilly Circus, until dawn came up over London.

What a night!

John Blake's exclusive interview with bad boy Keith — Page FIFTEEN.

The legendary Stones last night: Ronnie Wood (left), Ollie Brown, Billy Preston, Mick Jagger and Keith Richard.

LOVE-TIFF YOUTH IN

SLIGHTLY MADDOCKS

2
Some Girls

Some Girls

★

The start of the Stones adventure

I don't want this book to just focus on me and Ronnie. It's not the story of our relationship but, obviously, meeting him was the start of this amazing adventure.

My relationship with Ronnie began, like lots of the best things in life, at a party.

I got home from a shoot one day really tired. I wanted a night in and a bath, but my mate David rang me and asked whether I'd like to come to a party he was throwing.

I can always find a bit of energy if there's a good party to go to, so I told him I was up for it. I dragged my friend Richard with me, thinking, 'What the hell, I'll probably know everyone there anyway.'

I just stuck on my Granny's dress – I was into vintage even then – and a Harris tweed jacket and some beige boots. Thinking about it, I could wear that outfit now. I went along to David and his wife Lorraine's house on Sheffield Terrace, in Kensington, and there were loads of interesting people in the room. Pattie Boyd was there, Bill Wyman too, and as I looked around the room, I saw Ronnie.

He walked straight up to me and started chatting. He just came out with the line, 'Do you know who I am?' and then whipped out a copy of the Stones album *Black and Blue*, pointing himself out on the cover!

I knew who he was, of course, but I wasn't a massive fan of the Faces or the Stones, so I didn't really know that much about him.

I just thought, 'Oh my god, this guy deserves to be put in his place for being so full of himself.' He asked what I did, so I told him I worked at Woolworths, in the main branch on Oxford Street. He looked a bit surprised and asked if I was in management and I was like, 'Nah, I work on the broken biscuit counter.' Me and my mate Sue always used that line with blokes who were trying it on. If they were still interested when they thought we worked shovelling biscuits, then maybe they were worth thinking about.

I wasn't bothered about him being famous. I was modelling and I'd already met loads of well-known people. It was also very different then. There was no big deal about being a celebrity – the word 'celebrity' wasn't even used – and no one was in awe of fame like people are now.

The thing that got me about Ronnie was he was very funny. He kept following me from room to room, chatting away. When I went to get a drink, I looked in the mirror above the kitchen sink and I could see Ronnie in the reflection of the mirror and he was jokingly pretending to hump me from behind! I thought, 'This guy is absolutely nuts,' but I thought he was really funny too. He was just silly and I suppose I was as well – in some ways he was like a male version of me. I had never been out with anyone who looked like him.

Anyway, he left in the end and I stayed the night at my friends' house and went out to work the next day. When I got back that night, there was Ronnie

Meeting Ronnie

An excerpt from my diary, the night
I went to *that* party.

sat in the front room. It turned out he had been
outside Woolies for a few hours waiting for me to
finish work. My and Sue's story about the broken
biscuits had clearly worked a treat. He didn't seem
to mind too much and we picked up where we'd left
off the night before. We just clicked straightaway,
got on really well and started to hang out together.

We saw each other constantly for a couple of
weeks but then he went off to New York. I wasn't sure
if that was it but then he called from America and
invited me to Paris, where the Stones were going
to record an album. He said, 'Meet me at a place
called L'Hotel on Friday.' I managed to find out where
L'Hotel was, turned up all excited and asked for
Mr Wood's room number. The man on reception
looked down at me and said, 'We 'ave no Meester
Wood 'ere, mademoiselle.'

I couldn't believe it. I felt so stupid. I was in Paris
with no money, no hotel reservation and no way of
contacting Ronnie. I kept on asking the receptionist
to double-check but in the end I had no option but to
admit to myself Ronnie wasn't coming and to ask for
a room for the night. The receptionist shook his head
and told me they were fully booked because of the
Prêt-à-Porter Fashion Week. I couldn't believe it.
I must have looked so desperate that he took pity on
me because eventually he said I could stay in one of
the maids' rooms. He led me to this tiny little space
at the top of the hotel – it was the smallest room
I'd ever seen. I was lying there all night thinking,

'How the hell am I going to get out of here? I haven't
got any money, I'm going to have to leave my bag and
pretend I'm off sightseeing, oh god...' At 6am I get this
phone call from reception.

'Is that Mademoiselle Karslake?'

'Yes, I mean, oui.'

'Are you also known as Mademoiselle 'Oward?'

'I am.'

'We 'ave a Monsieur Wood down 'ere asking for you.
Shall I send him up?'

'Yes, that would be wonderful.'

I quickly dressed, stuck on my sarong and, before
I knew it, there was Ronnie at the door with a big
smile on his face. I went straight into his arms and he
started to apologize, saying Concorde had blown an
engine so they'd had to make a landing in Shannon
in Ireland. While he's saying that, some other bloke
shoves past us into the room. He didn't even look
at me, just sat on the floor at the end of the bed,
rummaging in a doctor's bag.

He pulled out a silver spoon, a bottle of pills and
a lighter. In a few seconds he'd crushed one of the
pills, heated it into a liquid, filled the syringe and then
injected himself straight through his jacket. There
was a tiny pause while the drugs hit his system and
then he looked up at me with this big grin and said,
'How very nice to meet you, my dear. I've heard such
a lot about you.'

And that's the story of how I met Keith for the first
time and our friendship began.

27

1977 October

Sat Sun Mon Tue Wed Thu Fri Sat Sun Mon Tue Wed Thu Fri Sat Sun Mon Tue Wed Thu Fri Sat Sun Mon Tue Wed Thu Fri Sat Sun Mon
Oct 1 2 3 4 5 6 7 8 9 10 11 12 13 14 15 16 17 18 19 20 21 22 23 24 25 26 27 28 29 30 31

5 Wednesday

Week 40 (278-87)

Went to Paris

arrived at hotel at 1·30 No Ronnie
finaley went to bed, woken at 8
6·00. RONNIE ARRIVED

with Keith
they flew in on
concorde but it
broke down so they
stopped in
shannon

Meet Me in Paris

★

Keith and Ronnie came as a package. When they arrived in that tiny room, we just stayed up all day chatting and drinking, and God knows what time we went to bed. I woke up in the middle of the night, hugging Ronnie, and Keith was there, asleep at the end of the bed. We were in that room for God knows how long and Keith suddenly said, 'Let's go to my apartment.' I couldn't believe he had an apartment and we'd all been sleeping in these maids' quarters.

We got there and Keith made this big fuss that we must have his bedroom. I found him fascinating. His sense of humour was, and is, brilliant. He loved us all to go to Fouquet's, this really posh restaurant on the Champs-Élysées. We'd go there having had no sleep or food for days. We'd realize we were starving and Keith would say, 'Let's go to Fouquet's.' We must have looked such a motley crew.

Keith was just very naughty. He had his Bentley, which we used to drive around Paris in. It was a very different time then, and it's hard to believe now that drink-driving didn't ever occur to us. We'd just get in the car and drive off at seven in the morning after a night in the studio.

First shot
. . . .
Another page from my diary, when
Ronnie arrived in Paris. The picture is
our first Polaroid together.

Some Girls

This is my copy of *Some Girls*. I don't need to play it –
I was there when it was recorded.

November 1977

Tuesday **29**

(333-32) Week 48

Ronnie has 5days off.

November

...ednesday

...nt to Nassau.

FUNCKY NASSAU

R.W. 1978

Christmas doodling

A Christmas drawing of the two of us by Ronnie, and a page from my French diary with some of my drawings. I always loved to doodle – I still do.

December 1977

Sunday 25

HAPPY CHRISTMAS AND A PROSPEROUS NEW BUNKET

26 jeudi
Ste Paule
26 339

semaine 04
janvier

Me lover just bought this diary for me + its lovely am sitting at keefs after have gone shopping for racing car sets and gotta Doll for mums Birthday bit early But better early then late went to Expencive food shop, Bought lots of goodies for keef to eat which we Ronnie paid for love my lover. x

My punk birthday
....

I designed this invite for my 23rd birthday. The cover doesn't reflect the words inside, which say, 'Punk gathering', but when you look at the pictures, no one is dressed up, and my only contribution was my plastic trousers.

you ar invitad to...

Jo's 23 RD

bAnG yOuR 'EAD oN tHE 'WALL, cUr YouR wriS+s , bursT yA VeINS, rüiN yA nose ,

PUNK gAtHERiNG

And after at LocAL FRenCH HosIptAL.

P.S. PUNK EVeNiNG WEAr ESSENTIAL!

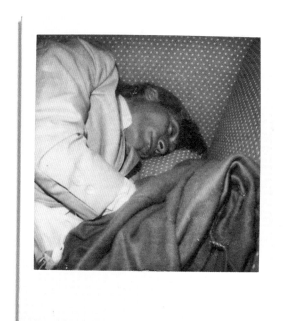

14 mardi
Ste Mathilde
73 292

semaine 11
mars

Ring Mum with
address & phone number

semaine 11
mars

mercredi 15
Ste Louise de Marillac
74 291

JOSEPHINE'S 23RD BIRTHDAY

LEFT FOR L.A.
SLEPT ALL DAY AFTER PARTY

BIRTHDAY PARTY AT APARTMENT.

WOKE 3:00 in MORNING PACKED
EVERYTHING TO GO TO L.A.

LA, baby

Things were moving so quickly.
No sooner had I had my party than
we were on our way to Los Angeles.

3

The Rolling Stone Life

The Rolling Stone Life

★

Living with the band

Ronnie and I had only been together for six weeks when I found out that I was pregnant – with our daughter Leah – which was a complete shock and a total joy. We decided that we would make a go of it and moved to Los Angeles because the Stones were touring over there and it seemed the right place to be for Ronnie's career.

The other big thing was Keith had to get off heroin. He'd been using it for a long time but he'd got busted and he knew that if he didn't give up, they'd put him in jail. The band were due to go on tour and they were rehearsing in Woodstock in upstate New York. Keith decided that was where he'd go straight.

It's amazing how determined he was. He went through this cold turkey that was like having a stinking flu for a week but he stuck at it. At the end of it, he emerged like a butterfly from a cocoon. It was incredible to see; he was funnier, happier and cooler than ever before.

I remember the first thing he wanted to do was meet a girl. He'd never shown any interest before but, once he was clean, he suddenly asked if I had any mates I could introduce him to. I actually knew someone called Lil, who was doing some modelling in New York, so I called her and invited her up.

She was keen, so Keith hired a chopper and just flew me to New York to pick her up – that was the way things were. They got on like a house on fire and went out with each other for a couple of years.

The Stones went off to tour *Some Girls*. I went for a few of the shows but, because I was pregnant, it was decided it was too risky for me to be flying everywhere and so I went back to this house we'd rented on Forest Knoll Drive in the Hollywood Hills. It was such an LA house, with a swimming pool in the living room, something I'd never seen in Benfleet!

After the last couple of shows on the *Some Girls* tour, Ronnie came back to the house with Keith. He moved in with us and lived there for a few months.

We bought somewhere in Mandeville Canyon and Keith moved in there too. He realized there was a little guesthouse in the back and thought, 'That'll do for me.'

He was living with us until just before Leah was born. In fact, the day Leah was born, Keith came to the hospital as well. The nurse asked which of Ronnie and Keith was the father and they both said, 'I am.' God knows what she thought.

We didn't see that much of Mick in LA – he was always on the move – and Charlie and Bill stayed in England. Charlie's wife Shirley had horses, and Bill never liked to travel unless he absolutely had to. I love looking at the pictures from this time, with everyone so relaxed.

Life in Los Angeles was great. My son Jamie came to live with us, we had baby Leah and this beautiful house in Mandeville Canyon. There were always loads of interesting people around. It was while we lived there that Ronnie met John Belushi. The Stones had been playing *Saturday Night Live* in New York, and when Ronnie came back, he had a new friend who we loved hanging out with.

He was a special person, John. He used to make me laugh so much, and I have such great memories of him. He had a bit of a crush on me. One night after we'd been drinking all day, Ronnie fell asleep on the sofa. John turned to me and said, 'Run away with me, Jo!' I told him, 'You must be mad, that's my boyfriend lying there,' but I told him I loved him anyway. I really did love him, he was one of a kind, and I was devastated when he died.

Proud parents
....

This is me and Ronnie on the hospital bed in Los Angeles the day I had Leah. I think I look pretty good, considering.

Partying in LA
....

Below: A random Polaroid from LA.
I always loved to dress up.

Opposite: We'd just moved into
Mandeville Canyon and we're wearing
crowns because we were the king and
queen of our new home. To the right is
our Prince Charming.

LA life

Opposite: Singer Harry Nilsson, Ronnie and actor Seymour Cassel.

Right: This Polaroid shows Keith, Ronnie and me in Forest Knoll Drive. Note the HP sauce on the table. It went everywhere with us.

Muddy Waters

....

The Stones played a show in '81
with the blues legend Muddy Waters.
He was a hero to the boys and they
were honoured to be a part of that
night. I only wish I'd taken more
pictures. It was such a great gig,
in a tiny club – the Checkerboard
Lounge in Chicago.

1. "I'M A MAN"
   (Mick, Keith and Ron with Muddy)

2. "THINGS WON'T BE THE SAME"
   (Keith & Ron with Buddy Guy)

3. "HOOCHY KOOTCHY MAN"
   (Mick, Keith & Ron with Muddy)

4. "LONG DISTANCE CALL"
   (Mick, Keith & Ron with Muddy)

5. "THIS UGLY WOMAN"
   (Keith, Ron & Ian S., with Lefty Diz)

6. " WHEN I GET HIGH"
   Mick, Keith, Ron & Ian, w/ Muddy)

....

This was taken on tour in America in
'81, just before the band went on stage.
I love this picture of Mick. He looks
lovely, really natural.

Downtime in LA

Above: Legendary drummer Jim
Keltner, Mick and Ronnie in our front
room in Mandeville Canyon, Los
Angeles. That's Ronnie's stereo Jim
is playing with.

Right: I bought Ronnie the sax for
Christmas and six weeks later he
played it on his solo album.

In the Studio

★

Going into the studio totally changed the way I listened to music. Before then I just listened to it as a whole and never thought about the different elements that went into a song. Seeing the Stones record in the studio was like learning how music actually works. I'd see them listening back really intently to what they'd recorded. At first I thought, 'What are they listening to?' and then slowly I was able to work out, 'Ah, there's Ronnie's guitar', or 'This is Bill's bass overdub', or 'That's Keith's riff.'

What I found really fascinating was when Mick came in. I'd have heard the music come together but would find it really difficult to imagine how Mick would sing over it. He'd listen really closely and it was just amazing the way he was able to put his words on top of the music and make a song. I said to him once, 'How do you find the song you're going to sing?' and he told me, 'Jo, I just take it as far away from the music as I can while still making it fit.'

Mick and Keith were always credited as the songwriters, the Glimmer Twins, but they all played a part. Charlie, Bill and Ronnie all put their bit in and it takes all of them to make it work. It's like a painting, each of them adding a colour. They spent so long perfecting what they wanted to do. I never found that boring – there's a lot of hanging around but you've got music and they were always having fun. It was fascinating. I stayed in the studio all night long. In the early days I built a little club room with a notice on the door saying 'Jo's Club', and I'd have drinks and joints ready for Ronnie and Keith when they took a break.

We didn't use to finish in the early days until 11 in the morning but that changed in the later years. Mick didn't like the all-nighters. He tended to go in late afternoon and would sometimes finish before dinner but the rest of them would go through the night. Mick would just go in to do his bits at the end. He found that easier. He's a more social person and wants to work during the day and be able to go out for dinner. Keith just wants to be in the studio playing his guitar and he wants his playmate Ronnie with him. Charlie doesn't care, he'll do whatever.

Leah is born

....

Below: Me doing a Demi Moore when
I was pregnant with Leah. The other
shots are during and after the birth of
our girl.

22 **vendredi**
St Maurice
265 100

semaine 38
septembre

1.55 ~~a.m.~~ in the morning
BABY WAS BORN.
♥LEAH. MICHELLE♥ 7 lbs 3 gr
21 inches long.

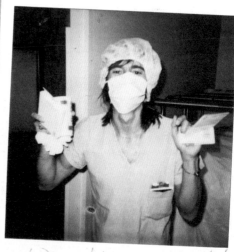

Dr Whood!!

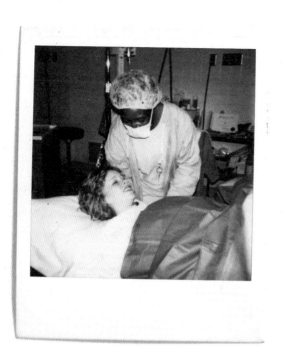

Family life

Right: Leah getting fatter.

Below: Me with Leah and Jamie in LA.

Opposite: A beautiful drawing Ronnie did of me in '79.

Ronnie Wood
3rd September

CUSTOMER'S COPY

fiorucci

07191

DATE _____

BY _____

206 NO. BEVERLY DRIVE
BEVERLY HILLS, CALIF. 90210
(213) 550-1938

DESCRIPTION	AMOUNT
	A 553 5 137.50 M2
	A 595 5 31.90 M2
	A 13 39 45.00 M2
	A 7K
	001 8874 10/26/79 251. CHRGL
	251. CHRGTO
	001 8874 3 1040/79
	47.72CHRG

NO REFUNDS

NO REFUNDS WHEN SUBJECT TO EXCHANGE OR CREDIT. MERCHANDISE
MUST BE RETURNED IN ORIGINAL CONDITION WITHIN 7 DAYS
ACCOMPANIED BY SALESCHECK. EVENING WEAR
AND BATHING SUITS MAY NOT BE EXCHANGED.

VISA	M/C	AMX

SIGNATURE _____

CUSTOMER
NAME _____

ADDRESS _____

CITY _____

Velvet wardrobe

....

Left: This receipt from my favourite store is from the late '70s. I used to dress Ronnie in quite a lot of stuff from here, especially my velvet jeans, which I had in pink and blue.

Below: I always loved taking pictures of Jerry Hall, and this is one of the first.

Like father, like daughter
....

Right: From the time we were on holiday in Jamaica and my daughter is copying her father. By the way, it was unlit!

Below: With Bob Geldof.

Ronnie

Ronnie, asleep with a beer and his beloved saxophone. It had once belonged to Plas Johnson, who played the original *Pink Panther* theme. The Stones sax player Bobby Keys found this rare instrument for me.

John Belushi

....

John had fallen off the wing of a plane when he was making the film *1941*. He needed some pain relief and our friend, 'the crooked dentist', was always happy to write a prescription for Percodan. John is being really silly with my vitamin pills in the Polaroid to the left. He threw them all in his mouth, laid on the floor and said, 'Take a picture.' As you can see from the other photo, we were always mad together.

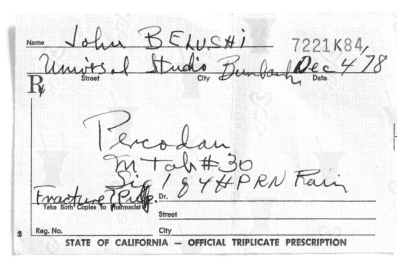

New camera
....

Not only did I have a Polaroid but
Ronnie also gave me a new camera,
which I could take these beautiful
pictures on. I love this picture I took of
Ronnie, and the lighting is wonderful.
We were in Nassau and the band were
recording *Emotional Rescue*.

Family dress-up

Left: This black-and-white picture of Jamie, Keith's son Marlon and me was taken by my good friend Jane Rose. The band were having a serious meeting with their manager Prince Rupert Loewenstein and we just shuffled in as an alien mummy and her two children. I said, 'Come along, children' in this silly alien voice and the whole place was silent. We shuffled out pretty quickly but no one minded.

Opposite: Charlie and me with Leah, my darling son Jamie, and below, Jamie and Marlon dressed as twins.

Nassau

The picture opposite at the bottom
is one of my only photos of Bill's
former long-term partner Astrid, with
Mick and Jerry cuddling on the couch.

Christmas with the Stones
············

The somewhat cheeky joke on this Christmas card was suggested to me the year before by Eric Idle as he tried to tempt me back to his. I didn't accept his invitation but I never forgot the joke. Ronnie drew the brilliant card and we sent it out to all our friends in Los Angeles.

Opposite: Keith wrote me the top note at Christmas after I threw him out of the guesthouse. It wasn't personal but he had to go. I'd just had a baby! The note below is the IOU for the birthday present he said he was going to give me one year. I can't say I've ever had any interest in firearms, but the thought was there.

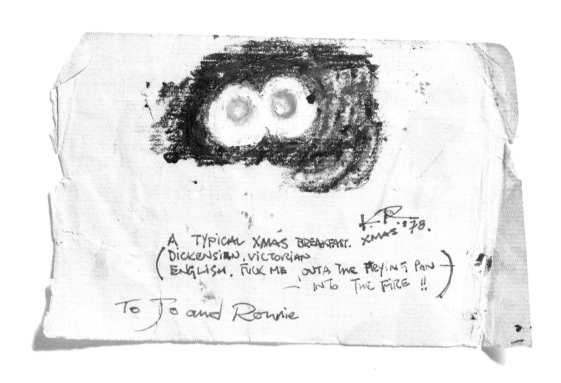

A TYPICAL XMAS BREAKFAST. XMAS '78.
(DICKENSIEN. VICTORIAN
(ENGLISH. FUCK ME . OUTA THE FRYING PAN
— INTO THE FIRE !!

K.R. '78.

To Jo and Ronnie

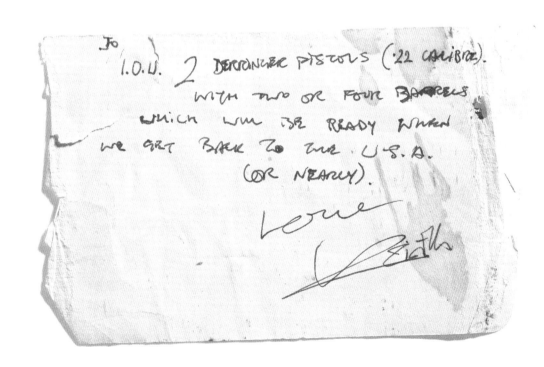

To
I.O.U. 2 DERRINGER PISTOLS (.22 CALIBRE).
WITH TWO OR FOUR BARRELS
WHICH WILL BE READY WHEN
WE GET BACK TO THE . U.S.A.
(OR NEARLY).

Love
Keith

fumes and stains on wall.

VEIW FROM BED

Blocked in window

STONE BED

6

bars

long wall + high

Ronnie

to outside

Now its sunday we have both been here since friday an experiance never to forget friday night was the worst [after having spent ages in police offices] finally was put in a tiny cell which stunck to high heaven with piss, then a stone shelve along one side for the bed, and a small red bucket, hadnt seen Ronnie for couple of hours the boss said he was on the other side werever that was anyway was later to find out. They took my jewellrey, all except my heart round my neck which they let me keep on after I shed a few tears asking them when I could see Ronnie and what about my kids. so my first night in st maarteen jail was the worst, no book, no

back to sleep again till 9.00 when they bought salami in bread again and what is it with the salami jamie would love it in here. and also a cup of coffee, so then started talking to all the guys and reading and a bit of writing today I met Doris who is so funny I laughed & laughed with him in fact today was quite funny with the lads malcombe talked a lot to Ronnie he does this by taking the dustbin to approx were his cell is and stands on it then he can look over the wall down onto Ronnie and thats how his been able to speak to anyone well only to him. Message from Ronnie today dont eat the meat and he loves me and I love him too ♡ after lunch which was rice with everything in it,

Jailbirds

★

This is my diary from the time I spent six days and six nights in jail. They were the longest six days of my entire life. It's a long story. We'd gone to St Martin in the Caribbean with the kids. The idea was that we'd have a healthy holiday but one night we went to a casino and met these guys called Franco and Mustapha. They gave us a joint and we had a bit of a chat with them.

St Martin is not exactly a big island and they found out where we were staying. A couple of days later they knocked on the door. It turned out they had lots of particularly good cocaine and the healthy holiday went right out the window. We stayed up all night and, at six in the morning, they asked to borrow our rental car to drop off one of their mates.

They came back, returned our car and left. We didn't think anymore about it but later that day I looked out the bathroom window and there were all these police in the garden. Ronnie thought we had the music on too loud but they swarmed into the house, arrested us and took us off to jail. I was locked up in an awful cell with a concrete slab to sleep on. They gave me this charge sheet and the only words I recognized were 'opium' and 'trafficking', so my heart sank.

It turned out that Franco and Mustapha were big-time dealers and when they borrowed our car, they'd picked up a huge bag of coke. For some reason they'd stashed it in a tree in the grounds of our place. A security guard saw them and reported them to the police.

We didn't know any of that and I was told horror stories by the other prisoners that I'd be inside for months. Eventually, our lawyer got us in front of the judge. He was very stern and asked me if I'd taken drugs. I put on my innocent face and said I'd tried them for the first time that night. He gave me a very stern talking to, told me off for being silly and then just let us go. No charges, no cautions, nothing! I think he realized we were just victims of circumstance. We were so lucky. How it didn't end up in the papers I'll never know, and if we'd been cautioned, it would have been really difficult to have a drugs bust on our records. I remember it made me really think and I said, 'I'm never going to do anything like that again.' And I stuck to that – for a few days at least.

4

On the Road

On the Road

★

Mad life on tour

It was a whole new world, going on tour. Me and my camera, off on an adventure. On the *Some Girls* tour, I was only there for a couple of shows, so my first big tour was with the New Barbarians. They were a band that Ronnie came up with so that he could tour with his solo album. He went to Keith and asked him to be a part of it, and he also got his old friend Ian McLagan from the Faces to join as well. Bobby Keys, the sax player who'd worked with the Stones, was there too and so was bassist Stanley Clarke and the drummer Zigaboo from The Meters.

It was a mad tour, which cost Ronnie loads of money in the end because he insisted on using private planes wherever we went. We were only in America, so we could have driven and he'd have come out with some money, but instead he ended up owing the record company hundreds of thousands of dollars. We had a great time, though.

I loved finding out what life was like on tour. In the early days it all seemed to be one big party and one big laugh and adventure. I'd be lying if I said I remembered everything – I look at some of the photos and have absolutely no idea where we were. I have to refer to what people were wearing, what my hair was like and how skinny I was to work out when it was. But I do remember having an awful lot of fun.

When Keith had gone to court for possession, he was sentenced to give a charity fundraising concert for the blind. He decided that he wanted to play the show on the New Barbarians tour in '79 and Mick came up and made a special appearance.

The Stones went back out on the road in '81, playing America after they'd released the album *Tattoo You*. They'd had a massive hit with 'Start Me Up' – they still start shows with that song to this day – and they were playing huge stadium shows.

Back in those days the tours were relatively short and our kids were really young, so they didn't come with us. We had a fabulous nanny and they stayed at home with her unless we were doing big shows like LA, New York or London.

Touring life was great. What I loved most was that you became like a family, but not just with the members of the band. It was all the people that never get a mention, like roadies and assistants, that I bonded with.

Ronnie's long-term roadie was a man called Royden Walter Magee but everyone called him Chuch. He was from Detroit and he was the toughest but sweetest man you could ever meet. I adored Chuch. He taught me everything I needed to know about being in the studio and, more importantly, being on the road. I had an amazing bond with him – sometimes just from a look on his face or a signal I knew what he meant. He taught me how to tune the guitars and pack them all away and where all the kit was backstage that Ronnie would need in case he was busy. He was so good to me.

Then there was the lovely Johnny Starbuck, who worked backstage. Chuch was with Ronnie until the day he died in 2003. We were in Canada and he said he was going to have a nap. He was found dead on a flight case with the guitars underneath him. He'd had a heart attack. He was only 54 but he lived life to the full. Johnny took over from him.

There was also Alan Dunn, who I am still very fond of, and he's a really close friend even now. He was Mick's personal assistant and he looked after logistics. He'd been with Mick since the beginning and, again, he was just part of life on the road and knew how to make it fun. When the boys were on stage, we were always having fun and laughing.

I hope the pictures on the following pages give a taste of what life was really like on the road.

Rocking out

Hamming it up with one of Ronnie's guitars backstage on the tour in America in '81.

Back to Paris again

These Polaroids were taken in the apartment that we rented just off the Champs-Élysées in Paris. We went back there a few times when the band recorded at the Pathé-Marconi studios.

Behind the lens

This is the first 'posh' camera that Ronnie gave me. I loved it so much we took selfies in the mirror to get photos of us with it.

The early tours

Right: Keith backstage
between songs.

Below: Bill Graham, the famous
American promoter, doing up
Ronnie's laces.

New Barbarians

A few mementoes from the
New Barbarians tour, including
a little good luck note from Mick.
How I saved that, I just don't know.

Atlanta Gazette May 6, 1979

Alex Cooley Presents for 96 rock

The New Barbarians

Featuring

Ron Wood
Keith Richards

With

Stanley Clarke
Ian McLagan
Joseph Modeliste
Bobby Keys

THE OMNI

Thursday, May 10 8:00 P.M.

$9.50, $8.50 & $7.50

Available at all S.E.A.T.S. outlets, All RICH'S, ALL metro area SEARS in Atlanta, Gainesville, Rome and Athens, OMNI INTERNATIONAL (Mon thru Sat), PEACHES, OXFORD SHOP, Griffin and CUSTOM SOUND in Athens. TO CHARGE TICKETS CALL 577-9600

CONCERT HOT LINE: 261-KOOL

---

12 Part IV—Mon. May 21, 197   Los Angeles Times

Polans

COOPERATION—Ron Wood, left, and Keith Richards share a spotlight at Forum concert.
Times photo by George Rose

A KICK IN OERDRIVE

New Barbarians— 'Happy Together'

"We're not gona lead you on with any guests. We're happy to have the band together," announced Ron Wood halfway through the New Barbarian concert, Saturday at the Inglewood Forum.

That might have disappointed those who were anticipating appearances by some of Wood's prestigious cronies, but, in an almost defiant tone, Wood's warning placed the focus where it belonged—on the rollicking rock of his temporary alliance.

Wood is ostensibly the leader of this tour—designed to support his LP "Gimme Some Neck"—but the cooperation between Wood and another potential distraction, costar Keith Richards, contributed to the evening's rollicking relaxed spirit.

Wood wisely refrained from trying to overshadow his Rolling Stones cohort—a classic rock 'n' roll figure whose heroic presence and crisp playing were consistently gratifying. The prevailing tone was closer to the party-time spirit of the Faces than to the mystique and drama of the Stones, as the principals seemed intent on having their fun and giving the crowd its money's worth.

The repertoire—including Wood's solo material, a couple of Stones numbers and some venerable blues and rock 'n' roll selections—was a bit uneven and repetitious, but the band kicked each song in ...

1979

Friday

138-227 Week 20 PAY
Last Quarter

OFF—

1. SWEET LITTLE R + ROLLER
2. BURIED ALIVE
3. F.U.C. HER
4. MYSTIFIES ME
5. INFEKSHUN
   LOST + LONELY
6. ROCK ME BABY
7. LOST + LONELY
8. BREATHE ON ME
   SURE THE ONE
9. LOVE IN VAIN
10. LETS GO STEADY
11. APT No 9
12. HONKY TONK
13. WORRIED LIFE
14. I CAN FEEL THE FIRE
15. GROOVIN YOU
16. SEVEN DAYS
17. WALK BEFORE / RUN
18. J.J. FLASH
19.

T F S S M T W T F S S M T W T F S S M T W T F S S M T W T F S S M T
1 2 3 4 5 6 7 8 9 10 11 12 13 14 15 16 17 18 19 20 21 22 23 24 25 26 27 28 29 30

To Keith + Ronnie
Good Luck.
Love Meck

81

82

New Barbarians

Opposite: I designed this red t-shirt and also came up with all of the words on it. Ronnie drew the guy and I posed, so he could get a good likeness of a bottom. The sleeves and bottom of the t-shirt had jagged lines and the words 'Cut along dotted lines' – which is why it's cut like that. There's also a great selection of Polaroids from the tour here too.

Stones on stage

....

This is how I mostly viewed the shows, from behind the amps, looking out at the massive crowds.

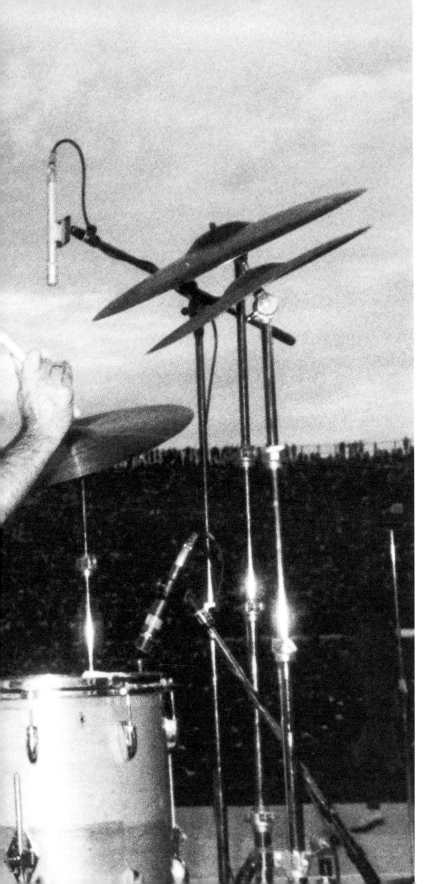

Drummer boy

I love this pic of Charlie. It looks so dramatic and cool – and he's got a little smile on his face.

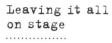

Leaving it all on stage

....

Opposite, far left: A classic pose from Bill – he always held his bass upright like that.

Rolling
Stones X2
TUNING
ROOM

Backstage Life

★

I love my backstage pictures. There was always a buzz there, an incredible sense of anticipation. That atmosphere didn't become jaded in all the time I was with the Stones, and the excitement levels before they went on stage never dipped. I think that's because the massive importance of the show being great never changed.

Everyone was really focused on doing their bit. Whether you were a roadie or worked in wardrobe, we were all part of a team, and everything came down to the show being fantastic.

The backstage area was the band's little sanctuary, where they got their heads together, prepared, did the set list and saw people. You never knew who was going to turn up but there was nearly always someone interesting. People were always desperate to get backstage passes just so they could be part of that world. They could be old friends or big stars, artists, sportspeople or film stars. People were always drawn to the Stones, so I always wondered who was going to be in that night. Later on, we had politicians turn up as well – it was a sign that things had changed when you had Presidents and Prime Ministers, such as John Major, turning up to a Stones show.

Socializing only happened before a show, really. The minute the show was over, the band were in the cars and out of there, back to the hotel or straight to the plane, so before the gig was when you'd meet people.

There'd be a lounge where all of the guests would gather and each of the band members would have their own dressing room, so they had some privacy and could get away if they had to.

I'd go to Ronnie and say, 'So and so is here. Shall I bring them in?' He'd either say, 'Give me half an hour' or 'Bring them in for ten minutes.' In '82, it was a bit of a free for all. There was no such thing as a meet-and-greet then – no one had thought of stuff like that. It was more rock and roll, and it was a lot of fun.

At first I was a bit timid about getting rid of people, but as time went on, I became Ronnie's little bouncer and had no trouble throwing people out. You'd get rid of them and the band would have time on their own, have a drink and then, boom, it was stage time.

Fun behind the scenes

....

These pictures show how much things have changed – they were taken on the '81/'82 tour, before the gigs became a real production. It was all quite basic and easy-going. In those days, Keith and Ronnie shared a tuning room.

Backstage pass

....

I love this image of the boys heading towards the stage. We were obviously in a stadium and they look like a couple of gunslingers.

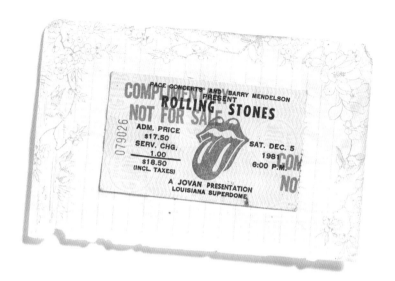

Getting ready

Ronnie's trick for making sure his hair
stayed up was to use fresh lemon juice,
followed by a blow-dry. To be fair to
him, it worked a treat – his hair stayed
right where he wanted it.

97

Mischief backstage

More goings-on backstage. I adored
Keith's jacket (below, top right)
– he loved a bit of leopardskin.

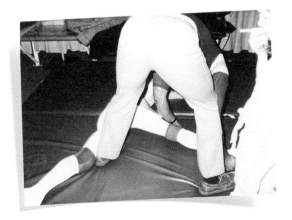

The tools of the trade

Opposite: When I got my things out of storage, I found the leather pouch that I used for keeping all of Ronnie's guitar picks in. Here's a selection of them.

Opposite, below left: Ronnie's Zemaitis, which had a metal plate on the front.

Below: Keith's guitar – it had his hat on it.

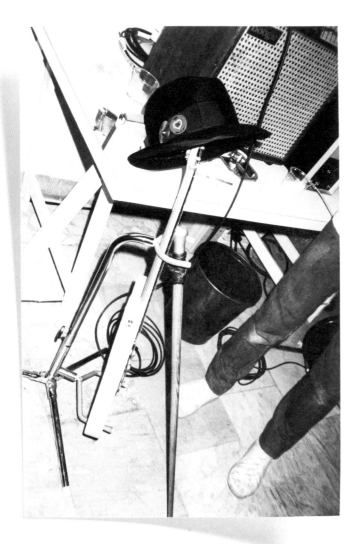

Stu: The Sixth Stone

★

Stu was the sixth Stone. He'd been with them from the very early days and he was hugely important to them. I think the decision was taken when they first came through in the '60s that he didn't look right to be an official member and, to be honest, I could see why. The rest of them were all crazy looking with long hair, whereas Stu looked more like the comic character Desperate Dan. He had this big chin and was a big stocky guy, who always seemed to have loads of stuff falling out of his pockets.

Although he was never an 'official' member, he carried on being their keyboard player and he also took on the role of looking after all the logistics, which was really important. When they were recording in Paris and needed to get all of their equipment to that studio, then Stu was the one who looked after everything. I think he was quite happy being on the sidelines. He kept himself to himself and I don't think he was remotely interested in dealing with all the stuff that fame brought. He didn't hang out, he didn't ever come back to parties, he was the grown-up.

He was very different from the rest of the band in lots of ways. He absolutely loved his food and playing golf, and back then those weren't things that were high on the band's list of priorities. It used to drive them round the bend because he'd book them into hotels that were out of town, where there was no action. He'd tell the band it was because they didn't want to be in the middle of the madness but they worked out that it was because there was a decent golf course nearby.

He was a lovely guy and always used to call me Petal. He was also a great player. It was a massive shock when he died and everybody was devastated. He was a young man and wasn't ill, and it all happened very suddenly. I think it hit Mick and Keith's relationship hard – he was a link between them and they missed him terribly. Also, he was such an important player that it took them a couple of years to work out what to do in terms of bringing someone else on board to replace him.

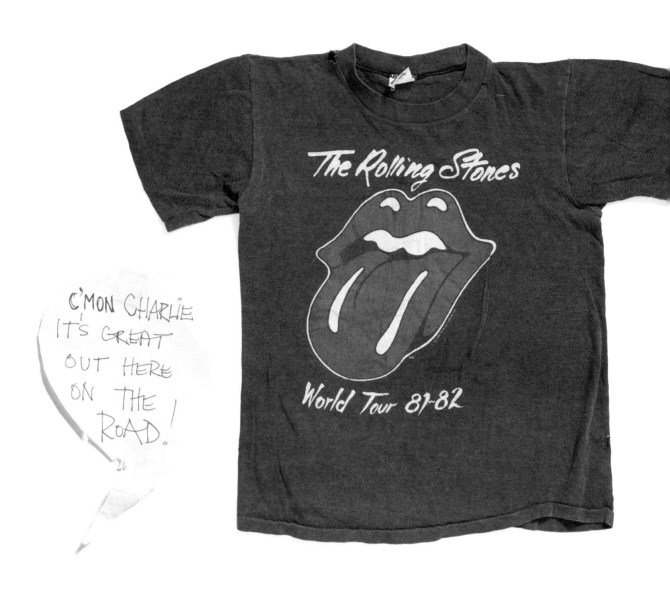

Life on the road

Above: The little note is from Ronnie to Charlie.

Opposite: I love the picture of Mick, he looks so cute, and the picture of Patti and Keith just captures a moment in time.

Travelling tales

....

Below: The snap at the bottom of the page is of the boys in the back of a limo. We always made sure the car was stocked with drink.

Opposite: Mick and Bill often used to play backgammon on the plane together – they used to have tournaments.

SUPERDOME
STONES 81
GUEST

136

computer generated **passenger ticket**

4 FLIGHT

TWA

More travelling tales

Below: This ticket was for when I took the kids back to Los Angeles ahead of the start of the tour in '81. The band had been rehearsing near Boston at a place called Long View Farm.

Opposite below: This shows the bedroom at the back of their private jet. Keith commandeered the room and he'd lie there as the plane took off. We'd all congregate on the bed once we were flying.

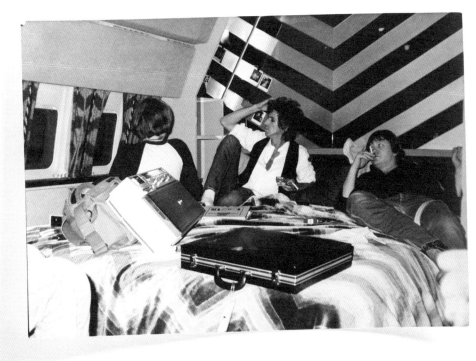

Just another hotel room

There seemed to be a lot of beige in the early '80s.

Ronnie kips
....

Ronnie asleep in an extremely messy
room. Note the sunlight coming
through the curtains.

Life on the road

Below: Ronnie among all
the luggage.

Friends on the road

....

Clockwise from top right: Ronnie
and Michael Cohl (the best promoter)
playing Boggle; Tony King (the Stones'
PR king) with Charlie's wife Shirley;
JC and Bob Bender, the security;
Johnny Starbuck and Bob Bender;
me and Chuch.

Kids on Tour

I have so many great photos of the kids on the road that it was incredibly hard to pick the ones that I wanted to use. I loved having my family on the road with us. It was wonderful, particularly when we'd go away for an extended period.

As I've said, when they were little, they'd only come to the big shows, and there was a massive gap in the '80s when the Stones weren't touring. Our youngest son Tyrone was born in '83, so he'd never seen the Stones play together until they went back on the road in '89. Everyone in the band had had more kids in the '80s, so it was great that they could all see what their dads did for a living for the first time.

When I look back, I think how fabulous it was for them – whenever they had a summer holiday, it was nearly always touring the world.

I said to them, 'If you're coming on tour, you have to look after yourself, you have to pack your bags and I'll come to make sure everything is ready to go when you're finished.' On the whole they were very good, although I do remember one time Ronnie and I came back after we'd been out for dinner. There on the room-service trolley was this massive empty tub of ice cream and a large tin of caviar. It turns out they'd been hungry and decided it would be fun to order some caviar on room service, followed by something sweet. We were like, 'What the hell, you can't just order caviar!' I dread to think what it cost.

But it was a great time because once Leah, Ty, Jesse and Jamie started to come out on tour, Keith and Patti decided to bring their girls, Theo and Alex, too. Then Mick and Jerry brought their kids, Jimmy, Lizzy and Georgia May, for the holidays and suddenly all the kids would hang out. We just became one big family and the children all have the best memories of being on the road. They loved it.

Time for family

Below: Ronnie and his Mum.
She loved a Guinness. Our
wonderful nanny Jaye Carter
is in the background. She was
with us for years.

Opposite: A fabulous picture of
Keith and his daughter Angela,
with Keith's good friend Freddie
Sessler poking his head in at the side.

Before and after
....

A shot of the stadium empty and
then how it looked when it was full.
Someone will know where this was,
of course.

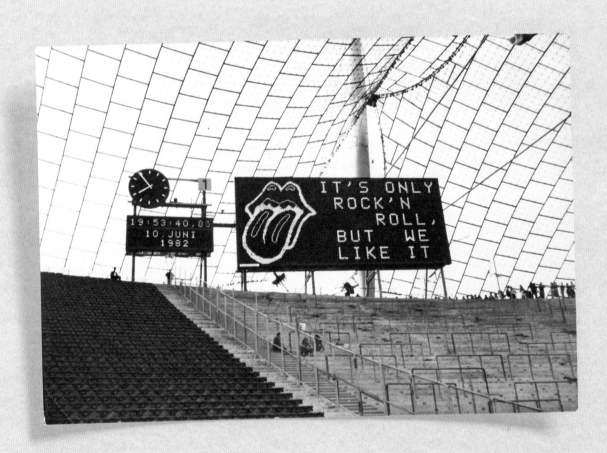

Watching the boys

I was always perched backstage, ready
for any event. The picture to the right
is a real favourite of mine.

Backstage vantage

These pics are taken from where
I nearly always stood – I hardly ever
got a photo from out front where the
audience was. The two shots below
were taken one after another. Ronnie
had come over to have a break for
a drink by Stu's piano and shouted
something over to me.

124

Dawn 'til dusk

The shows were always incredible. I really loved how they started off in daylight but ended at night because there was such a contrast. The energy built that way – the darker it got, the more excited the crowd became. The band liked it to be dark at the end because that way they could finish with a good firework display and the lights were really effective.

DIY fashion

....

Right: This pic shows Ronnie wearing a leather top with dots on it. I painted those on with Tipp-Ex but I thought it looked really good. You'd never know!

For the crowd

Ronnie used to have such a lot
of fun on stage. No matter how
tired any of them were, they could
always perform.

In the pit

These four shots were taken when I was in the pit. I started running around to hear certain songs from the front of the stage. The press photographers were normally allowed in there for the first two songs but after that it was just security.

Taking a bow

The end of another great show.

Crew hoodie

....

I dug this brilliant hoodie out of
storage and I didn't even realize
I had it. It comes from the end of the
'81 tour and it's signed by the band.
At the end of every tour we used to
get a commemorative t-shirt.

'She Was Hot'

....

These photos are from the set of the 'She Was Hot' video, the only video I managed to get myself into. I asked Mick if there was a part for me and he said, 'Let me think about it.' A bit later he said, 'Go to make-up tomorrow morning.' I thought, 'Woo-hoo! A sexy part in the video,' but when I went there, they made me up as the old wife of Bill Wyman. Thanks for that, Mick! I think this is the first time the guys had all worn the same suit, and you can see how much Keith was enjoying it.

'Too Much Blood'

On the set of the 'Too Much Blood'
video, which was shot in Mexico.

On set

I absolutely love the pic below of the four of them on the set for 'Too Much Blood'. But I have no idea where Bill was!

137

5

Time Out

Time Out

★

Most of these pictures were taken from our time living in New York. We moved to Manhattan in '82 after the Stones finished touring *Tattoo You* in Europe. Los Angeles was so mad that we decided the time had come to move out – it just didn't stop in LA, the craziest people were around us constantly. It was time for a change. Keith was in New York and he wanted his buddy there. Mick was there too, so off we went.

We found the lovely old brownstone house you can see in the picture on page 143, on West 78th Street. We just loved it there on the Upper West Side. It was a couple of streets down from where Mick lived and in a great neighbourhood. We dug out the basement and put a studio in, and we used to get all sorts of interesting musicians coming round to visit. David Bowie hung out, and also Bobby Womack and Don Covay, who both dropped by a lot.

We settled really quickly into being New Yorkers, the kids enjoyed school and I got pregnant with Tyrone. The following year Ronnie asked me to marry him, and we got married at the start of '85.

We did go out a bit while we lived in Manhattan – we went to places like Studio 54 and a hip little place called China Club – but we had young kids, so a lot of the time it was just about staying in and having people over. Ringo Starr and Bob Dylan and Sly Stone all came round. It was a really good party house, so everybody used to come back to ours. At Ronnie's birthday party, Andy Warhol was walking round with this camera he'd painted different colours, taking photos of people. He took a picture of me but I never took one of him. Damn! I wish I had! And I'd love to know what happened to his photos from that night.

The Stones were recording *Undercover* when we first moved there but there wasn't any discussion of them going on the road. Not touring meant we were a bit broke. I was never very good with money and Ronnie was even worse! But the good thing that came out of that is he started to work on his art again. I adored Ronnie's drawings and I loved sitting for him. He always had a pencil in his hand – he even drew me when I was in labour. It was another creative outlet for him and actually the first art form he really fell for – he thought he was going to be a sign writer until he became a musician. You can see some of his art in this book, and New York was where he started to take it seriously.

We were in New York for four years in the end. Looking back, it was a bit hairy. Now it's all safe and cleaned up but it was very different then. You had to be streetwise. It's funny because at the time I didn't go round thinking it was edgy, it was just the way New York was. I've never been one to feel afraid. It was a bit shady but the crime was just part of the city and you just lived it.

Where we were on the Upper West Side was pretty safe and we rarely went downtown. You had to be very careful if you did, and even then you could

get unlucky. I remember I was absolutely yearning for a curry and the only Indian place we knew was near Times Square. So off we went with all the kids and my friend Melissa. It was late afternoon, so you wouldn't think anything bad could happen. When we got there, Melissa went to the loo, which was on the floor below the restaurant. She was gone for absolutely ages. I couldn't work out what was going on and I was just about to go looking for her when the lift doors opened and there was Melissa completely drenched in blood and in shock. We all jumped up and started screaming for an ambulance. When she'd gone to the loo, there was some man who mugged her. Because the bathroom wasn't on the same floor as the restaurant, anyone could walk in off the street. He threatened her with a big piece of wood and demanded all her money. She gave him the $20 she had on her but, as she walked away, he whacked her twice with the stick anyway and split her head open really badly. I went to the hospital with her and they stitched her up but she was in a bad way.

When I came back in the early hours of the morning, Ronnie had already gone to the studio, leaving the kids with the nanny. I was in the house and heard a noise outside. I looked out of the window and there was this bunch of kids smashing the windscreen of a car. I opened the window and screamed at them, 'What the fuck are you doing?', and they looked up and held their knives up at me.

Shutterbug

Yet another camera.

That was it for me. The signs were all there, it was time to go home. We'd been talking about leaving for a while but it was at that moment the decision was made for us to move back to London. I missed my Mum and I wanted to bring the kids up in England. We also wanted to be closer to Jesse, Ronnie's son from his first marriage, and for the kids to all be together as a family. Also, Ronnie's parents were there. We just wanted to be close to family full stop. It really was time to leave.

We sold the house off for a crap price and hit the road back to London. Keith was furious we left, but it had to be done.

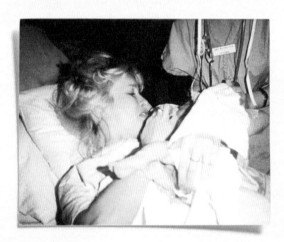

142

Living in New York

Above: This was taken outside our house on West 78th Street. From right to left, Bobby Womack, Don Covay, Keith, Ronnie and the kids.

Opposite: Top left is me pregnant in our newly decorated bathroom, which I designed. There's a photo of Ronnie wearing his favourite t-shirt and one of him reading one of his favourite books! The pic on the bottom left was taken just seconds after Tyrone was born, and bottom right is just after we'd brought him home.

Couples

★

I love looking back at these shots of all of us. We spent so much time together over the years and had a lot of fun.

I met Jerry before I met Mick. I worked on a commercial with his brother Chris for a French perfume – I played his girlfriend. We were supposed to be walking down a street and then Jerry walks the other way looking fabulous. The idea was that he couldn't stop staring at her because she was wearing this amazing scent and I was the furious girlfriend who dragged him away. She was already a famous model, who'd gone out with Brian Ferry.

We always got on, so it was great when she got together with Mick around the same time I started to see Ronnie. She was my first girlfriend in the band and I'm still very fond of her.

Patti came along in the early '80s and we bonded straight away. Keith told us he was seeing someone new and we went to meet her one night after the studio. She opened the door to her apartment wearing only men's pyjama trousers and jumped into Keith's arms with a big grin on her face. I thought, 'This girl is cool,' and she looked so beautiful. It's funny how certain moments in your life can stick in your head like a photograph.

I liked her immediately and I really admire her and Keith as a couple. They've been through a lot together and come through the other side. You can see in these photos how much they love each other.

Charlie and Shirley have stuck together through thick and thin. They've been a couple since the earliest days of the band and they are still together now. We didn't see an awful lot of Shirley on the road because she would be at home with her horses – she always had a life of her own – but she'd come to the big shows.

When I first got to know Bill, he was still with his partner Astrid, who he'd been seeing for many years. He was later married briefly to Mandy Smith, and then after he'd left the group he married Suzanne, which has been a long and happy marriage.

Mick and Jerry

....

Below: A beautiful shot of Mick
and Jerry with the Stones sax legend
Bobby Keys in the background.

Opposite: A rare shot of Mick with
a beard and some pics of the gorgeous,
fabulous Jerry Hall. The shot looking
down at the guys is taken from
a window at Mick's place in France.

Keith and Patti

....

Opposite: My beautiful friend Patti. I love these pics. She's an absolute stunner.

Right: Keith and his beautiful daughter Angela.

Below right: Keith serenading his 'little princess' Leah.

Below: An absolute favourite of mine of the two of them.

Wedding day

Just a couple of snaps of my wedding day. I loved the dress I designed. The pic below was taken when I got up and sang 'Then He Kissed Me'. I'm not a great singer, but I had Keith and Ronnie as my backing guitarists.

Holiday in Jamaica

We used to go to Jamaica a lot. This is one morning down at Laughing Waters and, boy, did we have a laugh Don't ask me why I was swinging out of the tree.

aggage Check

201446

Issued by

airJamaica

Kingston, Jamaica W.I.

The Original Bromance

★

Keith and Ronnie's relationship is the original bromance. They have been like brothers forever. I've got hundreds of pictures of them together, so it was very hard to choose which ones to put in this book, but I had to include one showing them just sitting together and playing. Whenever I think of them, it's always like that – wherever we'd be, they'd sit with their guitars and just play.

It's some form of meditation for them. I think it calms them down and they don't have to think about anything other than the song and the notes. It allows them to escape. Keith is always in charge of what they'd be playing. He is always the one in control, the big brother. You can see that from the pictures, I think, the way their relationship works.

Keith's an only child, so Ronnie is the closest to a brother he's ever going to have. He loves Ronnie and is always telling him off but they get on really well.

Those two hang out the most of any of the band members, and their relationship is very special. They could be angry with each other but because they can sit down and just play guitar, any arguments would be all forgotten. Well, at least while they're playing!

The boys

Whether we were in a hotel room or on holiday, like here in the Caribbean, the bromance continued.

Playing around

Right: When I think of Keith and Ronnie together, I think of how they look here. They are bonded by their guitars.

Buenos Aires
....

This was taken at our great friend
Luis Pastori's house, just outside
Buenos Aires.

Famous faces

....

We were never short of famous friends to hang out with. Clockwise from top right: Bernard Fowler (backing vocalist for the Stones), me, Ronnie, Sheryl Crow, Keith, Brad Pitt and Jane Rose (Keith's manager); Ike Turner and me; the back of a limo with Bo Diddley; a pick-up from Chuck Berry; Ronnie and me with Chuck Berry.

Famous faces

....

Clockwise from top right: Ronnie and
Jamie with Alice Cooper and Bernie
Taupin; Keith, Ronnie and me with
Donna and Dan Aykroyd; a Polaroid
selfie with Ringo Starr, his wife
Barbara, Ronnie and me; Peter Cook
with Ronnie and me; Kate Moss and
Jefferson Hack.

Famous faces

Clockwise from top right: Eddie
Vedder of Pearl Jam; me with
Kirsty MacColl; Ronnie and Keith
with George Thorogood; Peter
Wolf with a wig on; Kirsty MacColl
and her husband, music producer
Steve Lillywhite.

Jerry Lee

....

The wonderfully eccentric Jerry Lee
Lewis. This is us hanging out in his
trailer when Ronnie made a video
with him.

Famous faces

....

Clockwise from top right: with Eric
Clapton in '95; Ronnie and Slash;
Ronnie with Bobby Womack; Ronnie,
Rod Stewart and my friend Julie;
me with Ringo and Barbara in
New York; Ronnie, Keith and
Charlie with DJ Fontana.

Famous faces

From top to bottom: Ronnie and me
with the handsome Billy Idol; with
Phil Spector; Keith and Ronnie with
Johnny Depp.

163

Famous faces – and photobombing Keith

This page, clockwise from top right: Ronnie and Rod Stewart taking a selfie; Ahmet Ertegun with Leah and Lizzy Jagger; Ronnie and me with Robin Williams; Ronnie, Keith and Bob Dylan before they went on stage at Live Aid.

Opposite, clockwise from top right: Ronnie and me with Joe Walsh from the Eagles and his lady, Lisa; Ronnie and Aretha Franklin; Keith photobombing my photo with Aretha!; Keith and Ronnie with Stanley Clarke; Ronnie with Bo Diddley and Bo's bassist, Debbie.

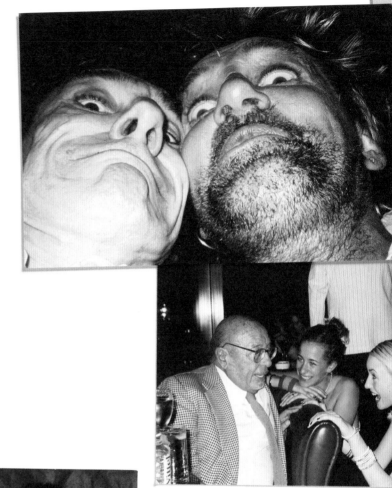

Joe
Walsh's
+ his
LADY LISA

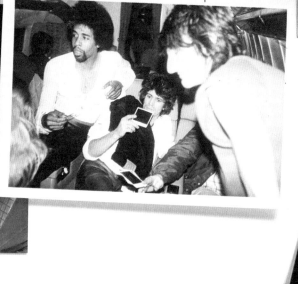

165

Keith having a laugh

Below: Keith's hand-written Polaroid.

Right: Life is just a balancing act
– Keith and Leah.

Opposite: Keith in a guitar box, ready
to rock and roll. Ronnie wrote the note
on the bottom.

TAKE ME UP
READY TO GO!!!

More Keith

....

Below: Who's behind the hat
and scarves?

Opposite: Keith and his Rasta hat.

Cassettes

★

Cassettes were great. It's funny because now everyone goes crazy for records but in the '80s we used to love cassettes just as much as vinyl. They were great because they were as portable as you could get. Someone would bring round a new album and we'd put it straight into the old tape-to-tape boom box and make a copy of it so we had it too.

Records were great as well but big, so you didn't want to carry them everywhere, while tapes were so much smaller and you could play them in cars and take them on holiday. As long as we had some cassettes and our big boom box, we had music, and music was essential for our life.

It's funny to think how handy cassettes seemed then, when you can carry all of your music on your phone now. We used to have a special case for carrying our cassettes around, which seemed very convenient at the time. We thought that was so amazing – until the Walkman came along, music was never portable.

I used to love writing on cassettes, and I was always cutting out pieces of paper to put in the sleeve or doing little drawings. I've got literally hundreds of cassettes in a box and, to be honest, I've just never been able to get around to sitting down and listening to what's on them. My brother played a couple and he discovered this hilarious message from an answering machine that Peter Cook had left. I should really go through them one day and see what else is on those tapes. Every night that the band were in the studio, they'd get a cassette at the end of the session, so there's probably loads of stuff there. One day I might sort them out...

Let the good times roll

Clockwise from right: Ronnie kissing
his brother Art; me and my bad habit!;
Patti and me dressed as waitresses
for the end-of-tour party, where the
band would wait on the crew; Keith
asleep on our couch after a long night;
another crew party with Lisa Fischer
and Cindy Mizelle, the backing
singers; Ronnie dressed as
a butler for the crew party.

Friends and companions

Clockwise from top right: Ronnie and me with Ronnie's brother Ted, Ronnie's son Jesse and Ian McLagan; Freddie Sessler and Keith; my lovely Alan Dunn in a kilt; Anita Pallenberg; Marianne Faithfull.

Recording in Montserrat

These pictures were taken by my
sister Lize McCarron when the band
were recording *Steel Wheels* in '89. It
was particularly memorable because
everyone had their kids there – you
can see them all on the veranda in
the shot opposite, in the middle.
Two months later, half the island
was destroyed by a volcano eruption.

Ronnie and donkey

We were on holiday in Mexico and
Ronnie had his first donkey ride on
an alcoholic donkey. You can see the
bottle of beer in its mouth.

Holidays and downtime

Right: Ronnie and our son Tyrone in the bath on holiday.

Below: in Jamaica.

Bottom: Mick and Ronnie on a boat trip in San Francisco.

To Ronnie Good. 'MY ASS TROW'

Karl Max. POPS

Rembrandt

Micheal Angela

HOGARTH.

SIR CLIFF RICHARD.

Stradivarious

HELEN SHAPIRO.

Adam Faith

(SIR GOVIA Z.U)

Serogin

CROW

Jaques Tati

Ri Wagner

RUBENS

(MOR AMON)

Van Gough
(EAR EAR)

Von Beethoven

the SPICE GIRLS.

Carrivaggio.

Amadeus

Titian
GUS DU preé Mozart.
Vermeer.
(ALL DOWN YER CHEST)

Sir Walter. Billy Fury.

L. de Vinci
Fies. A. Vivaldi.
(Tony the Wop)

J.S. Bach & Co.

Bridge

Canalletto.

Tooloose
Letrec

Yehudi
Menuin

Marilyn the Wop)
Monroe.

Gigli

Pavaroti.
with love

Archangel Corelli

Django
Rhienhart. Hayman.
(2½ FINGERS).
(KEEP IT UP)

ANT.

Nicknames

★

One day on tour, Keith handed Ronnie these three big pieces of paper. Keith was cracking up. He'd sat down and written all the names he could think of to call Ronnie – anything from Van Gogh to The Spice Girls.

Keith's a funny bloke and he does the maddest things but I think that's why I adore him. I don't know why the names are relevant but he thought they were hysterical.

He's done one for Mick as well saying , 'I love you', and then calling him Roger Daltrey, which is a wind-up. He's just very silly, and what I love about the nicknames is that it gives an insight into his sense of humour. Charlie's one has names like Louis Armstrong and Max Roach on it, which is because he's such a jazz fan.

When I was moving from my matrimonial home, I was clearing out the house and came across them. Ronnie had them framed years ago. I love them, they're a bit of fun and they always make me smile. They're just something to look at and enjoy.

Charlie Christian

Dizzy Gillespie

Carlo Little

Sly Dunbar

Gus Dupree

Joe Pass

Miles Davis

To Charlie

Ben Webster I V Dick

Earl Palmer (LOCAL 99)

Les Paul

With love,

Gerry Mulligan

Lester Young

Max Roach.

2000 Wes Montgomery

Philly J.

(STIX R US)

Tony Williams

C. Parker. (TOOTS)

Louis Armstrong

Georgie Wetling

Tito Puente

Gene Krupa.

Teddy Wilson

KEITH MOON.

Horsemouth (JAH)

Ginger Baker.

John Bonham

EDMONDO ROSS.

Baby Dodds.

(Bones & Skulls)

Stan Getz (A NICE BUNCH OF GUYS!)

2000 Oscar Moore.

Gerry Marsden

Gus Dupree

Al Jolson.

Billy Holliday. (STONED)

SPICE GIRLS. (WEE LUV U)

McKinley Morganfield.

Sir Cliffs

To Mick, you,

I LOVE

Roger Daltrey

Helen Shapiro

Herman.

Elvis Presley 2000.

Freddy & The Dreamers

Billy J. Kramer

Beryl Marsden

Pavarotti (Amore!)

Howling Wolf

Frank Ifield

Tina Turner

Marianne Faithful

Bobby Vee.

Donald Pears. (BHOBLING) BROOK

love Etta James.

KM 2000.

Frankie Vaughan

Patsy Cline.

Little Richard.

Blind Blake.

Cherry Wainer. (QUEEN OF THE ORGAN THE)

Liberace ☆

6

The Show Goes On

The Show Goes On

★

Back on the road

The Stones had been off the road for a long time by the time they toured again in '89. Mick and Keith had been doing their own thing and so had Ronnie. He ended up going off and doing things like touring with Bo Diddley and Titus Blues Band and painting instead. We had moved back to London and we were well into family life. We were still having a great time but it wasn't the same as being on the road with the Stones.

There was a bit of friction between Mick and Keith but, as Keith says, he and Mick are like an old married couple who will never get divorced. Ronnie finally got the two of them to talk to each other and that was the breakthrough. He was on the phone to Keith and then to Mick, encouraging them both to speak to each other, and the next thing I knew they were rehearsing. Suddenly there was going to be an album, called *Steel Wheels*, and we were going back on the road. It was very exciting to be going back on tour and there was a whole new vibe.

The Stones had a new promoter called Michael Cohl, and with his skills the boys went serious. It was amazing to how it compared to when we'd last been on the road in '82 – back then it was rock-and-roll madness. They were still playing stadiums, really big shows, but I used to do Ronnie's make-up and I'd bring his clothes to the show in a bag. It was all very loose. He'd wander on stage wearing whatever I'd brought to the gig. I don't remember anyone ever talking about curfews then.

One time we were woken by security because we were late for a show. I think that night the Rolling Stones were something ridiculous like four hours late going on stage. It was amazing that people waited. At the hotel I was running round desperately shoving our stuff into bin bags before we ran out of the door.

This time, Mick and Michael Cohl didn't want any of that chaos – now it was going to be a proper show. Mick came to me and said he wanted me to be Ronnie's personal assistant, which was great because it gave me a job that had to be taken seriously. I now made sure that we were packed and ready and that Ronnie was where he was supposed to be. I was going to do the best job I possibly could. Now there was a wardrobe room and a make-up room and everything had to run to schedule. Everyone had their own van for getting to and from the gigs – in the past, we'd all bundle in with Keith.

It was totally different by the late '80s, the industry had changed and the guys had to change too. There weren't any more free tickets, which we all complained about, and there was even an itinerary handbook with rules and regulations. We all laughed at the rules but we knew that change was upon us. We were sponsored by Budweiser, which meant we were warned not to drink other brands in public, although, to be honest, the boys didn't really drink out in public anyway.

Now it wasn't just a concert anymore – it had become a show, a production. When we saw the plans, there was this huge set with inflatables and towers and loads of flames everywhere. It was going to be amazing. The stage looked like a city, and then throughout the show there were loads of fantastic moments where things like huge inflatable dogs would appear. Now you only get massive events like that in Vegas, where the set stays in one place, but the Stones did it on the road. The stage was so big that they built three of them, so they could leapfrog each other as we went all around America. It was a huge success. The gigs were tighter, and Mick loved it when everything ran smoothly and more professionally.

It is bittersweet when I look back to that tour, though. It wasn't an easy one because I had a health problem that was misdiagnosed as Crohn's disease. I can see in some of the pictures that I'm not right but I just got on with it, and on the whole I had a great time.

We were away for so long and went to places for the first time. Japan was just fantastic. The audience was absolutely fascinating. At the end of each song they'd clap politely and then there was total silence as they waited for the next song. At the end, they would all file out in perfect order, row by row, it was so civilized. It was also the first time the kids came on the road and were old enough to enjoy it properly, and we all fell in love with Japan.

ROLLING STONES STEEL WHEELS

THE NORTH AMERICAN TOUR 1989

Rules of the Road

★

This is my copy of the handbook from the *Steel Wheels* tour. I loved to draw on it, making it mine. This book was our source of all information – there was no need to ask people where we were going or which hotels we were staying in, it was all there. We always made sure the kids had one, so they had our number at any time – of course, we had no mobile phones then, so that was important.

You can see overleaf that the book stresses, 'We all need to work together in harmony,' and the emphasis was really on being professional. We started to get a per diem then, which meant that everyone had enough money to cover themselves individually. Laminates always had to be used, it was a lot less casual. We really had become a proper production. It was the start of the tours becoming much longer, and it was all about being organized. We had to put out of our heads that we were going to be away for so long and take each show as it came.

STEEL WHEELS AMERICAN TOUR '89

A FEW POINTS FOR YOUR GENERAL INFORMATION AND WELL BEING...

THERE ARE A NUMBER OF RULES THAT WE RUN BY DURING THIS LITTLE EXCURSION AND YOU WILL BE RESPONSIBLE FOR HOLDING TO THEM.

1.   DUE TO THE HIGH PUBLIC PROFILE OF THIS TOUR, WE CANNOT STRESS STRONGLY ENOUGH THE NECESSITY FOR EVERYONE TO BE VERY AWARE OF THE U.S. AND CANADIAN LAWS RELATING TO THE CARRYING AND/OR USE OF ANY PROHIBITED SUBSTANCES. BE VERY, VERY CAREFUL IN PREPARING YOUR ENTRY INTO, AND CONDUCT WITHIN, THESE COUNTRIES.

2.   WE MUST ALL WORK TOGETHER IN HARMONY. REGARDLESS OF THE PERSONALITIES, CONDITIONS AND DEMANDS, WE MUST ALL STRIVE TO CONTRIBUTE 110%. THIS IS A PROFESSIONAL ENDEAVOR, AND SLACKNESS WILL NOT BE TOLERATED. REMEMBER THIS! IT WILL HELP YOU UNDERSTAND WHERE PEOPLE ARE COMING FROM.

3.   WHILST EVERY EFFORT HAS BEEN MADE TO HAVE ALL THE INFORMATION CONTAINED IN THIS SCHEDULE CORRECT AND ACCURATE, PLEASE REMEMBER THAT ALL THINGS ARE SUBJECT TO CHANGE SO DO CHECK WITH THE LOGISTICS DEPARTMENT IF YOU ARE IN ANY DOUBT. A NEWSLETTER WILL BE ISSUED ON A DAILY BASIS WITH TIMES AND TRAVEL / SHOW INFO, ETC, ETC.

4.   EVERYBODY ON THE TOUR WILL BE RESPONSIBLE FOR PAYING HIS OR HER OWN HOTEL INCIDENTAL CHARGES BEFORE CHECKING OUT. EVEN IF YOU HAVE NO CHARGES, PLEASE STOP BY THE FRONT DESK AND FORMALLY CHECK OUT AND RETURN YOUR ROOM KEY. IF YOU DO NOT DO THIS, THEN ANY CHARGES TO YOUR ROOM WILL BE DEBITED TO YOUR SALARY WITH NO RECOURSE TO THE TOUR.

5.   LAMINATED STAFF PASSES ARE FOR THE USE OF WORKING TOURING PERSONNEL ONLY. THEY MUST NOT BE LENT OR GIVEN AWAY. ALL GUESTS WILL BE GIVEN APPROPRIATE PASSES FOR EACH PARTICULAR SHOW. PLEASE REMIND YOUR GUESTS THAT THESE PASSES DO NOT GIVE BEARER THE AUTHORITY TO TAKE PHOTOGRAPHIC OR VIDEO REPRODUCTIONS OF THE SHOW.

GUESTS ARE NOT ALLOWED ON THE STAGE UNDER ANY CIRCUMSTANCES.

Continued Next Page.

The Steel Wheels rules
....

Here are some pages from the itinerary book we were given in '89 for the *Steel Wheels* tour. It was like our Bible.

6.   PLEASE OBSERVE THAT DUE TO THE RESTRICTED LUGGAGE HOLDS ON THE TOUR AIRCRAFT, ONLY 2 SUITCASES AND 1 CARRY-ON PER PERSON WILL BE ALLOWED ON BOARD AND, UNFORTUNATELY, THIS LIMIT WILL BE STRICTLY ADHERED TO. PLEASE TRY TO USE 'SOFT' LUGGAGE WHERE POSSIBLE AS THIS WILL HELP ALLEVIATE THE PROBLEM.

LUGGAGE CAN BE STORED IN NEW YORK OR LOS ANGELES IF THIS HELPS YOUR WARDROBE PLANNING FOR THE 4 MONTH TOUR PERIOD. PLEASE SEE ALAN DUNN FOR PARTICULARS.

7.   THE MAXIMUM TICKET ALLOCATION TO THE TOURING PERSONNEL WILL BE 8 (EIGHT) TICKETS PER SHOW, PER PERSON. THIS ALLOCATION WILL BE SUBJECT TO AVAILABILITY AND WILL BE ISSUED ON FIRST-COME, FIRST-SERVED BASIS. THERE IS NO SUCH THING AS A FREE TICKET. ALL TICKETS MUST BE PAID FOR AT THE TIME OF ISSUANCE.

AS TICKETS ARE ALREADY ON SALE AND MOST SHOWS ARE SOLD OUT, PLEASE MAKE SURE YOUR REQUIREMENTS ARE KNOWN TO SHELLEY LAZAR AS SOON AS POSSIBLE.

8.   THE CATERING FACILITIES AT EACH SHOW ARE FOR THE TOURING STAFF / CREW ONLY. THIS IS NOT A FREE RESTAURANT SERVICE FOR FAMILY, FRIENDS OR GUESTS. MEALS WILL BE SERVED ONLY TO PEOPLE WEARING A STAFF LAMINATE.

9.   THE SPONSORS OF THIS TOUR ARE BUDWEISER BEER IN THE UNITED STATES AND LABATTS BEER IN CANADA. IF YOU MUST DRINK BEER ON OCCASION, PLEASE BE MINDFUL OF OUR SPONSORSHIP RELATIONSHIPS AND TRY TO NOT PUBLICLY DISPLAY ANOTHER BRAND OF BEER WHENEVER PHOTOGRAPHERS ARE PRESENT.

10.   FINALLY, PLEASE REMEMBER IF YOU ARE IN DOUBT ALWAYS, ALWAYS, ALWAYS ASK - YOUR COOPERATION WILL BE GREATLY APPRECIATED.

WELCOME TO S.W.A.T. '89...

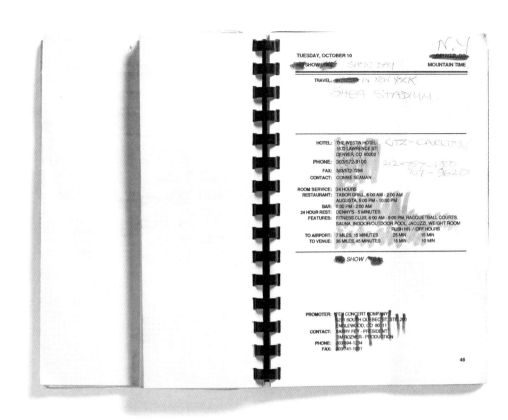

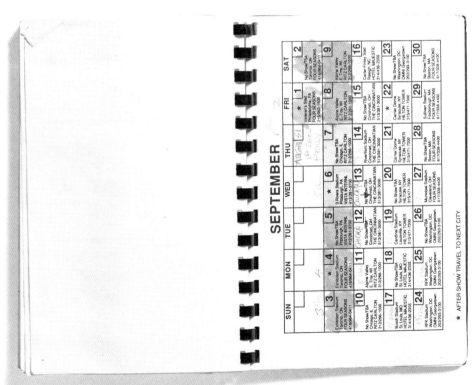

Back on stage

....

I don't remember when this was
taken but it could have been in South
America because the crowds there
went mad.

And back on the road
....

This page: I loved my Rolling Stones
Visa credit card! Below is a shot from
a video recording.

Opposite: Ronnie, Mick and me
in Japan.

193

The Stones in Japan

Right: With the kids in Japan, all wearing kimonos. Look at Tyrone doing a karate chop!

Below: The boys announcing the tour.

The calm before the stage

Right and below: Mick, waiting to go on stage.

Inset: The laminate is from Ronnie's solo tour in '92–'93.

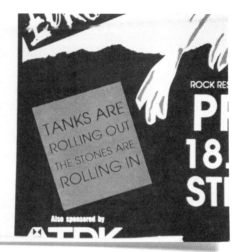

Fun backstage

....

Right: Jerry by Chuch's work station.

Below: Ronnie working on a set list.

Opposite, above right: Part of a poster advertising a gig in Prague shortly after the conflict there. We met the Czech President, Václav Havel, before the gig.

Opposite, below: Life on tour – Ronnie and me in Japan (left) and my sister and my kids (right).

Ronnie in Japan

Ronnie under the table, literally, after experiencing some very good saké.

Party time

This is an invite to Dan Aykroyd's party after the very first MTV awards. We took the kids to the awards show and went to the party afterwards – obviously.

Isaac Tigrett and Dan Aykroyd
request the pleasure of The company of

Ron Wood

at a small and private
late, late night / early morning supper
following
MTV's first Annual Awards reception
Friday Night / Saturday Morning
September 14/15

Upstairs (The Poor Boy's 21)
in the
Hard Rock Cafe
221 West 57th Street

Kindly RSVP as soon as possible
Use Members' entrance
THIS INVITATION IS NON-TRANSFERABLE

Times on tour

Some shots of life on tour from '89 onwards. The *Steel Wheels* tour was the last tour that Bill was on.

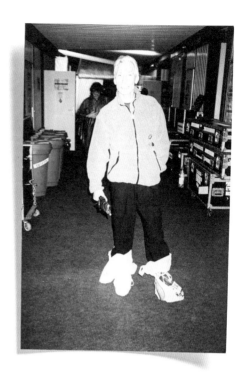

The Doctor is in

....

Opposite above: This was a sign for those in the know. When the Doctor (Keith) was in, you could knock on his door.

Opposite below: Keith had only a few requests on tour but one of them was shepherd's pie and HP sauce before a gig, which you can see on the table. That was what he ate every night before he went on stage, though he might only have a mouthful.

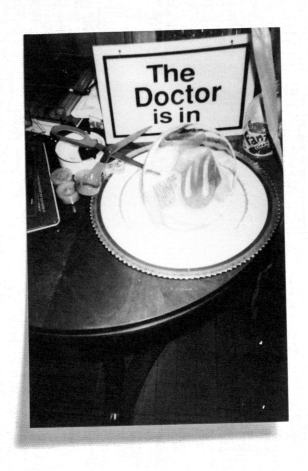

Birthdays

★

Birthdays were always a big thing on the road. The band would normally tour in the summer or just before Christmas, which meant there were lots of birthdays to celebrate because Mick was born in July, Keith's birthday is in December and Charlie's and Ronnie's are in June.

We'd always try to do something special to celebrate birthdays. This shot of Mick is typical of what would happen. If we were flying, there'd always be some sort of celebration on the plane. What I love about this photo is you can see the kids in the background. Tyrone is there looking up and he's so little – he can only have been about six or seven.

The difficult thing, of course, was buying presents for the guys. I'm really good at choosing presents but you can imagine how difficult it is to buy for somebody like Mick, Keith or Charlie. What do you buy a man who has everything and has loads of friends who are always giving him things as well? Something with a lot of thought. You have to think really carefully about what to get that they wouldn't just toss aside.

When Mick had a big birthday, there was always a really large party, but Keith was never the sort of person who liked a big deal being made over his birthday.

Birthdays on the road

Right: Keith's Mum Doris and his
son Marlon, celebrating one of
his birthdays.

Below: Ronnie with his guitar cake,
and a present I got for Mick.

Let It Bleed cake

....

Right: A replica of the cake on the album cover of *Let It Bleed*.

Below: A lovely thank-you note from Mick for the book I bought him one year.

J Jan—
en route to Panama

Dear Ronnie & J.,
Just a note to thank you for the wonderful book on the history of dance. Will peruse it when I get back at the end of the month. I hope you all had a great Christmas & New Year. I was in Mustique with all the kids + Jade + her kids + my Father below!
See you soon
Mick

Playing with Bob

I love Bob. He's such a fabulous man.
He's a Gemini, like Ronnie, but such
a different kind. Bob is quiet and an
introvert. We saw quite a lot of him
over the years. Whenever he was in
town, we'd go and see him. Bob toured
with the band in the late '90s and they
sometimes used to play his song
'Like A Rolling Stone' together,
which the Stones had covered.

Playing for Presidents

This is Ronnie playing at the
inauguration of George Bush.
In the photo on the right, you can
see the President, and in the one
below, Ronnie's stood next to
Barbara Bush, George's wife.

Back on the road

This cartoon is from '89 when the band announced they were touring for the first time in years. I ripped it out because I thought it was hysterical. Even now they're far from old.

"Everyone calm down. Walking frames shouldn't be this difficult."

Keith

....

This is Keith playing in Buenos Aires.
He just walked past me at the perfect
time and I got this great shot.

Costumes

★

Being a fashion-lover, I loved the stage costumes. I helped the girls in wardrobe, as well as being Ronnie's PA on the *Steel Wheels* tour and all the ones that followed. I loved the girls that worked there, so it was great fun and we were all part of a big team.

I loved getting Ronnie's outfits together, he's so easy to dress. His weight never went up or down, which he was always really proud of. He used to say he had hollow legs and that's why he could drink so much Guinness and not put on weight.

I used to go out shopping and find stuff for him, and I'd rip pages out of magazines if I saw something interesting. Later on, I'd take what I'd seen to the stylist in wardrobe and they'd have it made. This coat on the opposite page, for instance – I saw it somewhere, drew it out on some paper and went to see the stylist. They made it up for me, which they did with a lot of his jackets. Ronnie looked great in it. It was so interesting to think about what was going to work on stage.

All the band members have their own style. Charlie knows what he wants, so he was never too much bother. In his everyday style he's a classic English gent, very into suits – he once had a suit made to match his car. On tour it's about nice simple clothes that are easy to drum in.

Keith has a Keith style. He had this pair of black jeans that he sprayed with silver paint every gig. For some reason he would never have them washed. He would just spray them again and again until eventually he got a rash on his legs and then the jeans had to go into the wash. Many years ago, Keith used to wear Anita's old jackets, so he had that very rock-and-roll '70s look, which is still copied today.

Mick works very closely with a stylist, and as long as the clothes Ronnie wore didn't clash with Mick's, everybody was happy. Bill had that late '80s look going on. Around this time was Bill's last tour. It wasn't a shock that he left because we always knew he hated travelling. If he could take the car rather than fly, he would – he has a fear of flying and is quite open about that. We were all sad when he went because it wasn't going to be the same.

SEPT 30th

"ROCK IN A HARD PLACE". VIDEO

SEPT 30th 89

MICK

SEPT 30th

'Rock and a Hard Place'

Polaroids of the clothes worn in the video for the single 'Rock and a Hard Place'. I tore the pages out of my *Steel Wheels* handbook. I styled what Ronnie wore, while the rest were done by professional stylists.

sept. 30th

KEITH

COAT AND
CREAM SCARF
RED/GOLD/GREEN ENDS

sept 30th

RONNIE

gloves. COAT.

CHARLIE

SEPT
30th

BILL

gloves

SEPT
30th

Lisa and Cindy

Fabulous outfits on the backing
singers Lisa and Cindy. I became
really close to Lisa, who was with
the Stones for many years, especially
after Cindy left to do her own thing.
She is the most wonderful, beautiful
person, inside and out.

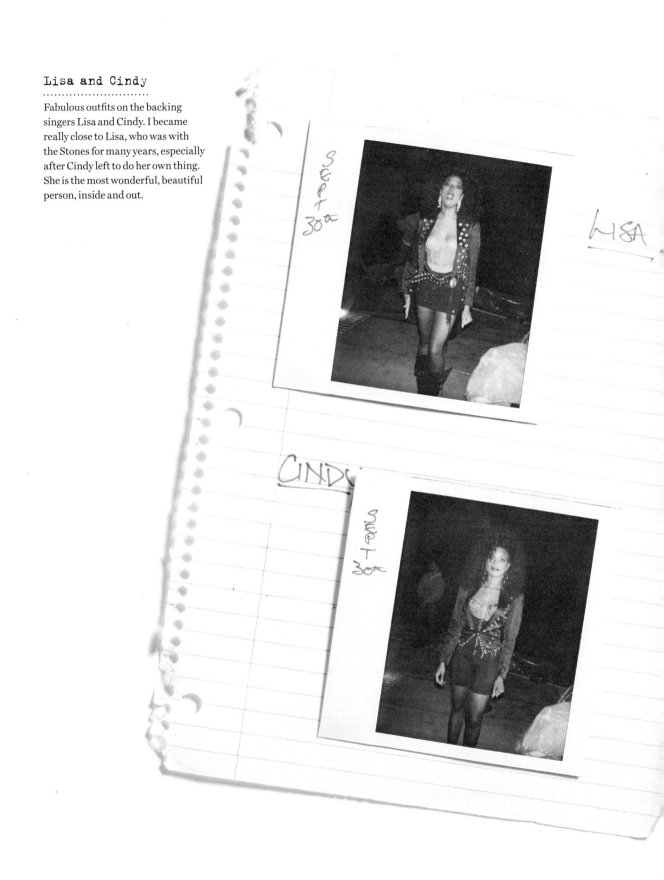

932:4200:076:898 :3

The Spin poems

....

This gives you a tiny idea of how much
luggage we used to travel with. On
the opposite page is a selection of
my luggage notes to Spin, who was
responsible for making sure it always
got to the right place.

SPIN.........ING WITH LUGGAGE

BAGS

HOUSTON  OKLAHOMA
JAN 27TH

SPIN

OKLAHOMA WHERE THERE IS
NO SNOW....
OKLAHOMA IS WHERE WE'RE
GOING TO GO....
OKLAHOMA WHERE WE'RE
GOING TO BE
ITS OKLAHOMA FOR ME....

THANKS SPIN

COUNT TODAY IS.....
6 BLACK CASES
4 GREEN BAGS
2 BLK SOFT BAGS
2 FLIGHT CASES
1 STEREO
2 GUITARS
1 BLK BOX

18 ♡ JO.

No.1

SPIN
SAN. FRAN — DENVER

RHYMES OF SENSE, I HAVE
NONE,
BUT I HAVE A RIDDLE JUST
FOR FUN......
IF LIFE IS HAPPY FOR ME
THEN WITH LIFE AS HAPPY AS
CAN BE
WHEN I SMILE AT PACKED LUGGAGE
TO THE COUNT OF 14
AND WRITE THIS UNTO THEE
IS THIS YOUR LIFE TO SMILE AND
JUST BE HAPPY AS YOU CAN BE...

7 THIS ROOM
7 THAT ROOM
PLUS VINI'S
PLUS LEAH'S

♡ JO

TOKYO °°°°°°° OSAKA. 18.3.03

O.K. SPIN. BULLET

WHERE DO I BEGIN....
THE AMOUNT IS SO VAST
BUT IT WON'T LAST
ITS FAMILY YOU SEE
ADDED ALL ON TO HIM + ME.

TODAYS COUNT. ♡ JO.

23

THIS INCLUDES FAMILY

No.

THE WESTIN

AS YOU SPIN THRU
ALL THE LUGGAGE
AND REQUEST OUR AMOUNT
OF BAGGAGE
I'M MISSING SOME OF
OUR TAGGIES
FOR MY 14 PIECES
OF BAGGIES!!......
THATS IT LOVE J

MELBOURNE  BRISBANE ☼

2ND MARCH .02.

HEY SPIN......

THE NUMBERS
THE SAME,
THE PLACES
ARE DIFFRENT
AND SO IS THE
PLANE !!!!

17

6 BLK SUITCASES
2 SOFT BL

ZAGREB

THIS LABEL YOU WILL FIND
SIX............. TOO.
ZAGREB THEY DO GO.
THEN THE OTHER 9 PLEASE
FIX...............TOO
LONDON I KNOW YOU KNOW
LEAVING ME WITH JUST
TWO......   TOO
PACK THAT THE VERY LAST
STUFF THEN BLOW

NEW YORK 19.1.03
°°°°°°°

TO CHICAGO.

Spin — THEY CAME
THEY PLAYED
THEY CONQUERED !!

NOW LETS GOOOOO

18 AS USUAL

♡ JO

2 GUITARS
2 FLIGHT CASES
1 STEREO
4 GREEN BAGS
6 BLK SUITCASES
2 SOFT BLACK
1 BLK BOX.

BOSTON
TO
N.Y.C.

O.K. SPIN
LETS BLOW THIS BOSTON THING
LETS GO ON THAT PLANE
TO NEW YORK THATS INSANE

WITH 18 BAGS.

2 FLIGHT CASES
2 GUITARS
1 STEREO
1 BLK BOX
2 BLK SOFT
6 BLK CASES
4 GREEN

♡ JO

The art of the room key

I would always draw on our hotel keys because everyone's looked the same. It was really easy to put them down on a table and then you wouldn't know which one was yours. I got into the habit of trying always to draw something different on every one of them. It's funny the things you learn on the road.

223

Tour life goes on

An original t-shirt I kept from '89.

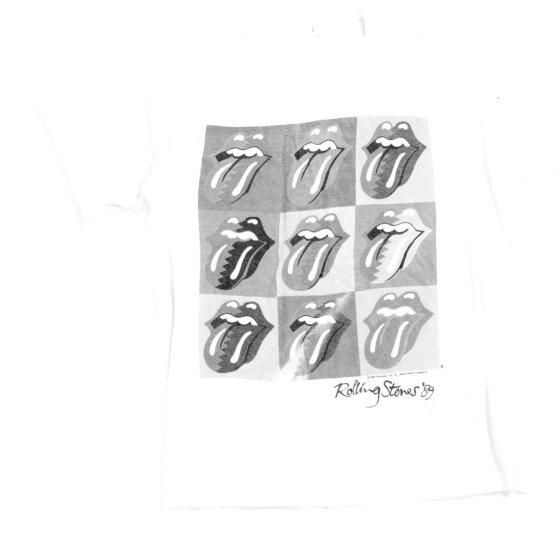

Tour life goes on

A denim jacket from the *Voodoo Lounge* tour.

Keep on Rolling

Keep on Rolling

★

Still having fun

In some ways, things didn't change a lot after *Steel Wheels*. One thing that did change was that I got better and better cameras, although I'm not sure you can tell from my pictures! Seriously, though, Darryl Jones replaced Bill and from that point on we toured regularly for years.

I got better and better at packing and started writing incredible baggage notes to the lovely Spin – the luggage guy who looked after everybody's cases. You can see some of them on page 221.

The Stones did so many tours after *Steel Wheels* that they all sort of blur together in some ways. I remember leaving my house in England, ready to go on the road, and looking around the front room and saying, 'See you in a year and a half, we're off on another adventure.' You can't think about the fact you're going to be away that long – you've got to think of it as another adventure.

And it was always an adventure. You got back into being with your touring family, and as time went on we took the kids as well. Leah sang back-up for Keith every night on one tour.

Once I got into the rhythm of being away from home, I found life on the road enjoyable. I was seeing the world, surrounded by people I loved, and the band were making so many people happy by doing the shows. Whichever city we went to, we would know somebody there, so it was always an opportunity to catch up with old friends. Touring became so natural.

As time went on, I became obsessed with organic food because it had helped cure me of my misdiagnosis. By the late '90s, I had designed a portable stove, which went everywhere with us, along with our 19 cases, which contained everything imaginable! We brought our own pillows, pictures of the kids (which were always on the bedside tables), and Ronnie had his own sound system. We basically had the contents of a small apartment on the road with us. When we'd arrive at the hotel, the first thing I'd do was spend time turning our room from a boring, beige space into something that felt homely.

Whether we were playing in Detroit or LA, the hotel room would have pretty much the same feel once I'd given it a makeover. Keith used to do the same thing – wherever he was in the world, you'd go into his room and it would look like his. There'd be candles lit, scarves over the lights and music blaring.

When you make rooms feel like that, you don't think you're in some strange place. Instead, you are at home wherever you are in the world.

While waiting for the luggage to arrive, I would nip off to the latest Wholefoods or health food shop and stock up on organic food. That way we didn't have to eat room service all the time. You do what you have to do to make the road feel like home.

I never found it difficult at the end of a tour to come home. I'd come back, make beans on toast and I could switch into normal life. It was much harder for Ronnie. He struggled to adjust because he'd miss the adrenaline and admiration that you got every night on the road.

I don't miss touring but that's probably because I still have a taste for adventure and love to go away and get out of my comfort zone. Among many places I've been to are Bangladesh and Tibet, and I even spent a month on a deserted island in the middle of the Pacific for a TV show with Bear Grylls!

Poolside in LA

Keith, Ronnie, Tyrone and Leah, relaxing by the pool at the Four Seasons in Los Angeles.

A Night in a Room

★

I absolutely love these pictures, especially the one opposite of Keith. He's laughing with all his heart, and it's a pure joy to look at.

This was such a good night but I can't remember where or when it was. I've asked Ronnie and he doesn't know. I then asked my brother Paul, who is in the pictures, and he doesn't know either. It's a mystery. I know it was the '80s, because my hair is curly, but other than that I'm none the wiser.

What I love about the pictures is that they capture what so many of our nights were like. We always laughed. We would hang out mainly in Keith's room. Vodkas would be poured, the guitars would come out, tapes would be played and hours would go by with music and laughter. Those nights were always about music and being with people you really cared about.

Seriously, though, if anyone knows where this was or where the cat came from, then please let me know…

Can't stop the music

This picture is from a small gig
where Keith and Ronnie got up
and played – Keith on guitar,
Ronnie on washboard.

The good times still rolling

Right: I love this picture of Keith and Ronnie with their sons, Marlon and Jesse.

Keeping it in the family
....
Right: Bert, Keith's Dad. Keith took him along on tour and showed him the world. He was there all the time, he had his own van and his own seat by the side of the stage.

Not happy

I particularly love these two photos because I'm sure Keith and Charlie were making some joke about Ronnie, which he wasn't amused by. Charlie is absolutely cracking up, but Ronnie looks furious.

Ronnie's artworks

I want to thank Ronnie for allowing me to use some of the beautiful drawings he's done of me over the years.

Another night, another hotel...

....
...still having a great time!

244

Room service

We are having a lot of fun here.
The good thing about these pictures
is I actually remember where we were!
They were taken at the Four Seasons
in Los Angeles, where we always
used to stay.

Holidays together

We all went on a family holiday together in '98. Our families were so close that holidaying together was natural. We went all around the Caribbean, even sailing through a storm that lasted 12 hours. The kids were amazing and slept through it all, while we were up all night because there was no way we could sleep.

Relaxing in LA

This is back at the Four Seasons in LA, with lunch around the pool and just chilling.

Laid-back Keith

I love this picture of Keith. It's just
a really cool picture that completely
sums him up.

Backstage treasures
....

Here's a recent set list and a laminate from a show in 2014. The shot of the crowd at the bottom is from Buenos Aires, one of my favourite ever shows. The crowds there were always insane.

RS SETLIST   TOKYO # 3   March 6, 2014

1. JUMPIN' JACK FLASH
2. YOU GOT ME ROCKIN'
3. IT'S ONLY ROCK AND ROLL
4. TUMBLING DICE
5. RUBY TUESDAY
6. DOOM & GLOOM
7. RESPECTABLE (BY REQUEST) (w/ Hotai)
8. HONKY TONK WOMAN
9. SLIPPING AWAY (KR) (w/ Mick Taylor)
10. BEFORE THEY MAKE ME RUN (KR)
11. MIDNIGHT RAMBLER (w/ Mick Taylor)
12. MISS YOU
13. PAINT IT BLACK
14. GIMME SHELTER
15. START ME UP
16. SYMPATHY (PYRO)
17. BROWN SUGAR

ENCORE

18. CAN'T ALWAYS GET (w/Choir)
19. SATISFACTION (w/ Mick Taylor)

250

Access all areas

I always loved keeping hold of my laminates. These are from some of the more recent tours.

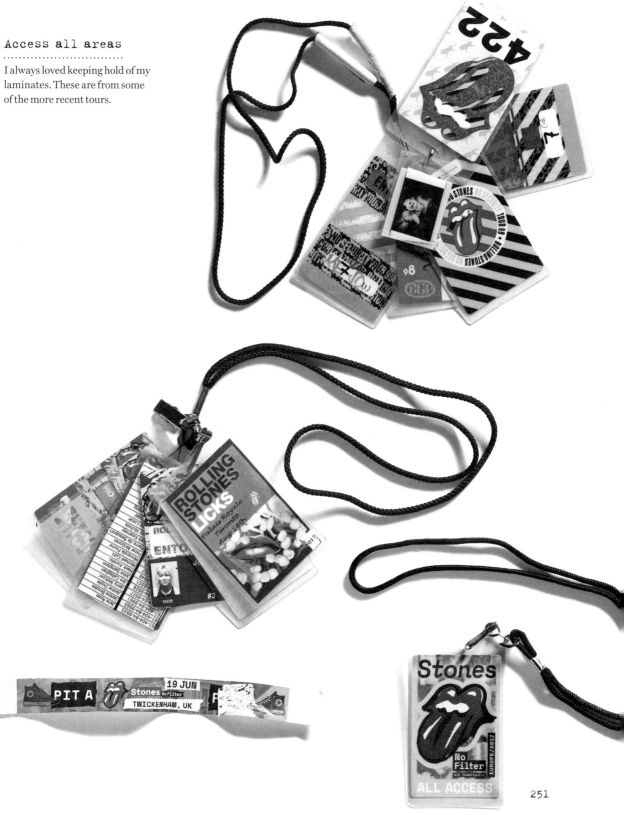

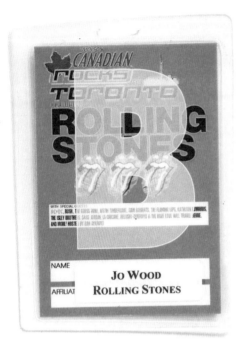

Passes and plectrums

Opposite: More backstage
passes from around the world.
The Rattlesnake Inn was the
backstage hospitality spot where
the great and the good congregated
on the *A Bigger Bang* tour.

Below: The Filthy Swine plectrum
was Keith's – he and Ronnie would
always think of different things
to put on their picks.

Acknowledgements

★

In loving memory of my mum and dad.

I would like to thank Jon Bennett who encouraged me to do
this book and was a joy to write with.

To my brother Paul Karslake for his encouragement and love.

To my family and my friends who love and support me.

And everyone who has touched my life.

A huge thank you to Jane Rose for letting me use
her pictures on pages 62, 147, 160, 238 and 239.

To my sister for her fab black-and-white ones on pages 174–175.

To Joe Cottington for believing in the book
and Ella and Jonathan at Octopus.

Kevin Pocklington at North Literary Agency.

Mark Wagstaff, Steve Fawcett, Dave Brolan and Emily DOLLY Sweet.

And finally to the boys in the band… it's only rock and roll!!!

Many thanks to Ronnie Wood, Keith Richards and Mick Jagger for kindly giving permission for their artworks, letters and notes to be included in this book.

An Hachette UK Company
www.hachette.co.uk

First published in Great Britain in 2019
by Cassell, an imprint of
Octopus Publishing Group Ltd
Carmelite House
50 Victoria Embankment
London EC4Y 0DZ
www.octopusbooks.co.uk

Design and layout copyright © Octopus
Publishing Group Ltd 2019
Text copyright © Josephine Wood 2019
Photography copyright © Josephine
Wood 2019

Text within images on pages 67, 81,
105, 166, 167, 178, 180, 181, 207
© individual copyright holders, used
with permission

Additional images:
4, 32b, 33a, 55, 66, 240, 241 copyright
© Ronnie Wood 2019
174–5 copyright © Lize McCarron 2019
62a, 143, 156a, 234, 235 copyright
© Jane Rose 2019
24, 30-31 Courtesy of The Rolling Stones
2 (background), 23 Associated
Newspapers Ltd/Shutterstock
20a copyright © TI Media Ltd 2019
81ar copyright © Los Angeles Times 2019
211 copyright © Charles Griffin for
Daily Mirror 2019

Every effort has been made to establish
copyright ownership of material
included in this publication. The
publishers ask to be contacted should
there be any errors or omissions.

Distributed in the US by
Hachette Book Group
1290 Avenue of the Americas
4th and 5th Floors
New York, NY 10104

Distributed in Canada by
Canadian Manda Group
664 Annette St.
Toronto, Ontario, Canada M6S 2C8

All rights reserved. No part of this work
may be reproduced or utilized in any
form or by any means, electronic or
mechanical, including photocopying,
recording or by any information storage
and retrieval system, without the prior
written permission of the publisher.

Josephine Wood asserts the moral
right to be identified as the author
of this work.

ISBN 978-1-78840-149-4

A CIP catalogue record for this book is
available from the British Library.

Printed and bound in Italy

10 9 8 7 6 5 4 3 2

Senior Commissioning Editor:
   Joe Cottington
Creative Director: Jonathan Christie
Editor: Ella Parsons
Editorial Consultant: Jon Bennett
Copy Editor: Helen Ridge
Photographer: Nick Pope
Production Controller: Emily Noto

Thank you to
everyone in the
Rolling Stones family!

And thank you for the
memories Shelley Lazar.